C o n t e n t s

KEY TO MAPS

✈   Airport

23   Road No.

⭐   Start of walk
     /drive

1250m▲   Mountain

ⓘ   Information

✝   Church

Introduction

Iceland is an epic land. Epithets like 'The Land of Fire and Ice' just hint at the delights this island has in store. Almost everything it has to offer is grand in scale, from its human history to its landscape.

Fishing for salmon

It is almost impossible to describe the beautiful and varied landscapes of Iceland without filling several pages. This is nature writ large – never boring, stark and strong, and always alluring. Vast cliffs, glorious beaches, the world's largest lava fields, glaciers, waterfalls at every turn, thousands of hectares of moors and tundra, and seemingly endless tracts of high desert plains only scratch the surface of what is on offer.

This panoply is further enhanced by the play of light and shadow that chases across the mountain ridges, moors and glaciers. It gives the effect of constant movement and induces an array of colours in mosses, heathers and rocks.

More fascinating than the surface beauty are the primeval elements at work just below. No matter what their age, humans cannot fail to be impressed by its super-hot fumaroles, powerful geysers and bubbling mud pools – this is our planet earth at its rawest and when faced with such monstrous power just below our feet we feel humbled and small.

Movement on land is mirrored by movement offshore and Iceland cannot be discussed without reference to its relationship with the sea. There are myriad languid coastal inlets, while the flotsam and jetsam of the Atlantic fetches up on beaches during winter gales and its waves pound incessantly all the year round at the base of cliffs in the Westfjords. The sea brought Icelanders to this land and its bounty sustains them to this day.

Iceland's human history is no less epic. A freedom-loving seafaring race driven from their lands by a ruthless monarchy, they made a living here through sheer grit and hard work, and then went on to develop one of the world's earliest parliamentary democracies. This is a people whose oral

GREENLAND
(DENMARK)

Arctic Circle

Reykjavik

ICELAND

NORTH ATLANTIC OCEAN

UNITED KINGDOM

Dublin

IRELAND

tradition was recorded as soon as quill and vellum arrived on the island, so we can follow every twist and turn in the fascinating narrative.

Today, after centuries as farmers and fishermen, Icelanders have embraced the modern age with gusto. With the help of technology – and particularly with the advent of the Internet – they are no longer a remote outcrop on Europe's northwestern boundary and the capital, Reykjavik, is one of the world's most 'happening' cities. Though small by international standards it has a strong vibe and is plugged into the modern arts like few others.

The slogan 'Pure Energy' probably sums up Iceland's appeal in the early 21st century. It is one of the least polluted countries in the world; most of its major attractions have been bequeathed by nature – a gift that keeps on giving; and most of its activities

The Vatnajökull glacier

are of the 'get out into nature' or 'high adrenalin' type that makes one feel refreshed and energised. Whatever feelings Iceland brings out in you, ennui will not be one of them!

Westfjords Turf House

The Land

Iceland has one of the most fascinating geologies in the world. Even a layman cannot help but be drawn to the elemental forces of creation at work here. Iceland is a newborn land straddling the European and Continental plates, and nowhere else on earth is the earth's crust as thin as it is here.

A view of the Southern fjords

The Great Misnomer

It was the Norse settler Flóki Vilgerðarson who named the country. After a rather easy summer, a sharp winter took him by surprise and all his animals died, so he cursed the 'Land of the Ice' or Ísland and the name stuck. But the most striking thing one notices even as the plane lands at Keflavik is the relative lack of ice on Iceland. There are volcanic flows, moors, sheer cliffs, meadows and deserts, but only 11 per cent of the land is covered the year round in frozen water.

The epithet 'Land of Fire and Ice' is more appropriate. Thirty per cent of the land is volcanic in origin and there are regular eruptions from several active volcanoes. The last major one occurred in 1996.

The youngest parts of Iceland, not surprisingly, are the highly active volcanic areas in the centre, southeast and the ridge running along the Reykjanes Peninsula. The Snæfellsjökull is just an infant, having only just been classified as dormant. This is really only a 'blink of an eye' in terms of geological time.

An iceberg near Fjallsjökull

Iceland

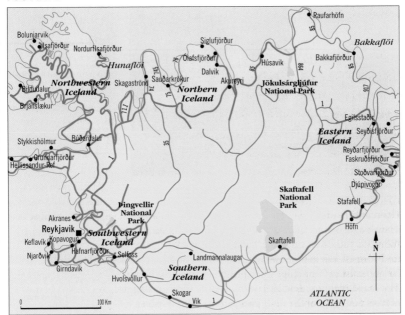

Landscape

Iceland's landscape is ever-changing and always impressive. Vast, dark and menacing magma flows, sheer cliffs, stark upland moors, pendulous scree slopes, active volcanoes, seemingly somnolent glaciers, geysers, steaming and smelly fumaroles, and black sand beaches – a true feast for the eyes!

Besides fire and ice, another factor that is elemental in Iceland's landscape is water. It is always on the move, sustaining spawning salmon in rivers or dropping in dramatic roaring waterfalls to the sea beyond.

Much of Iceland's landscape is magnificent and challenging rather than pretty, and much of it has never been conquered by humans. But where they have managed to gain a foothold,

neat farmsteads have sprung up, often in the lea of hills or in coastal knolls. Tiny Lutheran churches further stake man's claim.

A view of Lake Thingvallavatn

Icelandic sheep

Flora and Fauna

There's a joke in Iceland: 'What do you do if you find yourself lost in an Icelandic forest? Stand up!' The island is almost devoid of trees and most of the vegetation rises only a metre or so above the ground. But this wasn't always so. When settlers first arrived, up to 40 per cent of Iceland had a cover of trees and the timber was soon put to work as raw material for building houses and boats. What the Norsemen did not realise was that these trees were much slower-growing than in their native Scandinavia, and that their stocks could not be replenished. Grazing sheep further prevented regrowth and in a short time the forests were exhausted. Replanting programmes

began in the 20th century but over the last 30 years there has been an increase in concern about the depletion of Icelandic flora with pressure from grazing sheep, horses and reindeer, as well as soil erosion. The island's plant life is more varied close to ground level. There is a profusion of wild herbs including parsley, gentian, mint and mustard, and several berry species, while the lava flows are blanketed by a rich carpet of mosses and lichens.

Iceland is not rich in animals. When the colonists arrived there were only two mammal species– the co-dependent mouse and the Arctic fox. The waters are rich, with populations of fish, whales and seals but, without doubt, birds are Iceland's

THOMAS COOK TRAVELLERS ICELAND

This book is divided into a number of geographical areas. The capital Reykjavik is where you are likely to start your visit, and is a good place to get acquainted with Iceland's history, cuisine and nightlife.

Next comes a section on places around the capital covering many of Iceland's most famous and most visited attractions. You can visit these by renting a car or by booking one of the many well-organised trips that depart the year round. If you don't intend to tour the whole country, this section offers you a sampling of historical and natural attractions, to give you a flavour of Iceland.

After this we begin the journey clockwise taking in the attractions of the northwest, north, east and south. Iceland's ring road, Route 1, allows easy access between each region. Lastly we introduce you to areas 'Off the Beaten Track' for the least visited locations.

most abundant non-domesticated fauna. Large herds of introduced reindeer inhabit the uplands of the northeast of the island, and Icelandic horses and sheep are seen everywhere.

The Icelandic People

Much is made of the Viking legacy in Icelandic blood but it would be true to say that the population is less homogeneous than that. Simply look at a cross-section of the people and you will see that their hair colour runs from the Scandinavian almost-white/blond through strawberry-blond to brown. The same is true for the eye colour; a good percentage of the population does not have the blue eyes of the Vikings.

That is because, in addition to a Norse population, a number of Celts from Scotland, Ireland and the Orkneys were also part of the exodus fleeing the yoke of the Scandinavian monarchy along with their Viking masters – and their genes merged with those from Norway and Sweden.

Today, there are just under 300,000 Icelanders and all of them are descended from the very first 9th-and 10th-century settlers, making them one of the purest bloodlines in the world.

This information is not just of scientific interest but explains a lot about Icelandic society. Close familial and kinship ties forged over almost a thousand years of community living have recently been fractured by the modernisation of the Icelandic economy, and the mass migration from other parts of the country to Reykjavik. In 1880 there were only three towns on the island inhabited by just 5 per cent of the total population; the rest lived scattered around the coast. Today, two-thirds of all Icelanders live in or close to the capital and many farms have been abandoned.

An Icelandic fisherman

Soaking up the sun

The Ice Man Cometh: The Power of Glaciation

A glacier is a huge river of frozen water formed on land, built up over millennia of ice accumulation and lasting many thousands of years. It is one of the most powerful natural forces on the planet and plays an important role in shaping the landscape.

Today, around a tenth of the earth's surface is covered by glacial ice but during the Ice Ages up to 30 per cent can be subsumed. During the last Ice Age, the Pleistocene period, Iceland was almost totally buried under thick ice. Today, a tenth of the country's land area is covered by glacial ice and its landscape owes much to the power of these cold leviathans.

Glacial Erosion

Erosion occurs in two major forms. At the base and sides of the glacier, large amounts of rocky debris and smaller sediment are pulled from the surface of the land, held in place and carried by the constant thawing and refreezing of a thin layer where the ice is in contact with the land. This is called *plucking*.

In a second process, known as *scouring*, the aforementioned rocks and debris held in the ice are dragged over the land as the glacier moves down a hillside, scraping the surface of the rocks and causing marks called *striations*. When working at its most powerful, the immense weight, movement and

scouring of the glacier can reduce rocks to an extremely fine flour-like sediment which when mixed with water is known as *glacial milk*.

As erosion continues, a valley becomes deeper and wider over time, and takes on a characteristic U-shape.

Glacial Deposition

As a glacier retreats the rocks and other debris or sediment it carried down the valley are deposited on the land. The sediment can simply be dropped directly from the ice (*till*) or carried away from the ice by meltwater (*geofluvial deposits*).

When the till forms mounds or ridges it is known as moraine. A terminal moraine marks the farthest reach of the glacier. At the side of glaciers lateral moraines are deposited.

Jökulhlaups and Sandurs

In Iceland most glaciers sit atop active volcanoes producing unique glacial phenomena. The most dramatic of these is *jökulhlaup*, a sudden and dramatic release of glacial meltwater.

Jökulhlaups can be caused by gradual melting of the ice by subcrust heat. This process eventually produces enough meltwater to raise the glacial ice cap and the water drains away through the gap. However, a subglacial volcanic eruption can melt a large amount of glacial ice very quickly, causing an almost immediate flood.

Whichever way it happens, a *jökulhlaup* transport tons of soft sediment out from the glacier base, depositing it on an outwash plain as the surge loses its power. These plains, called *sandurs*, are specific to sites with subglacial volcanoes and the Skeiðarársandur in Iceland (from where the name *sandur* was taken) is the largest in the world. Up to 10m of sediment can be deposited on the *sandur* during one *jökulhlaup* event.

A characteristic *jökulhlaup* event took place during the Grímsvötn eruption in 1996. The flood built up over several days after the volcano let loose, giving scientists time to set up monitoring stations. The data collected contributed largely to the fledgling science of volcanology.

Facing page: The Fjallsjökull glacier
Above: The Hekla glacier

History

The history of Iceland has swung between periods of independence and subjugation. Since the end of the Second World War, the country has moved with the tide of the West and has been at the forefront of the NATO stance against the Soviet Communist republics. Its spirit and confident self determination has brought it into conflict with its neighbours and a worldwide 'green' movement.

A Christian crucifix

330 BC	Greek explorer Pytheas sails from Marseille to find the ends of the earth. He sails north past the UK and after six days comes across an island he calls Ultima Thule. It is believed that this was Iceland, but no records remain to confirm the theory.
c. 9th century AD	Irish monk Dicuil documents the travels of Irish priests to Thule – independent corroboration of the Pytheas text. Dicuil settles in Iceland but no long-term habitation is formed.
Late c. 9th century	Harald the Fairhead King of Norway, routs his enemies on the Scandinavian peninsula and harries them to the point where they set out to settle beyond his influence. Iceland, known to them as Snæland is a natural choice.
860	Flóki Vilgerðarson travels to the island, navigating with ravens (*see p6*). He is unimpressed with the place and nicknames it 'ís land' – literally translated as Iceland.
874	Norwegian Ingólfur Arnarson becomes the first recorded settler. A Viking fleeing the Norwegian choke, he farms land in an area he calls Reykjavik, or steamy/smoky bay.
930	The Icelandic parliament or Alþing is founded to govern the island by consensus. The Icelandic 'Age of Peace', also known as the Saga Age, begins.
985	Eiríkur the Red, father of Leifur Eiríksson settles in Iceland.

c. 11th century	Leifur Eiríksson discovers a new land to the west. He calls it Vinland. Modern theory has it that this was the east coast of northern US/southern Canada.	**1397**	The Kalmar Union between Norway, Denmark and Sweden (three independent nations under one Danish monarch) brings Iceland under Danish influence. The Union is troubled from the start.
1000	The Alþing declares Iceland a Christian country.	**1402–04**	Black Death ravages the island.
1056	Consecration of the first Catholic bishop of Iceland at Skálholt.	**1530s**	The Kalmar Union breaks apart as Sweden and Denmark play power games. When Denmark imposes rule over Norway it takes control of Iceland.
1118	The laws of the Alþing are written down for the first time. Also called the end of the 'Age of Peace'.		
1120–1220	The age of writing – the *Book of the Icelanders* is written at this time.	**1540–50**	Denmark imposes the Reformation on Iceland causing bloodshed and chaos across the country.
1230	The civil wars begin. Also known as the Age of the Sturlung after the *Saga* that commits the details to parchment. The political consensus begins to fall apart and private armies roam the land.	**1602**	Denmark enforces a trade monopoly on Iceland – goods can go in and out only through Danish companies and trading fleets.
		1783–85	Catastrophic volcanic eruptions wreak havoc across Iceland.
1262	King Hákon Hákonarson offers to help control the situation.	**1787**	Free trade is established in Iceland for Danish subjects but not for Icelanders.
1281	Iceland comes under the rule of the Norwegian crown.	**1800**	Abolition of the Alþing.

1800s	First stirrings of an Icelandic independence movement. Iceland-born figures such as scholar Jón Sigurðsson lobby for more commercial and political freedom.
1843	Alþing re-established.
1855	Free trade introduced for Icelanders.
1874	King of Denmark visits Iceland for the first time to mark the millennium of the foundation of the island. He declares a new Icelandic constitution.
1904	Icelandic home rule is declared under the control of Denmark.
1917	Women are enfranchised.
1918	The Act of Union recognises Icelandic self-determination as a state within the Kingdom of Denmark. The Act is to be reviewed again in 1940.
1940	Germany annexes Denmark. The Icelandic Alþing takes control of Icelandic affairs and declares the island neutral. The Allies are concerned that if the Germans take a

	defenceless Iceland they would control the northern sea approaches to the UK; so, in October, British forces occupy the island. They build the airfield at Reykjavik.
1941	British forces leave Iceland and American forces arrive.
1944	The Independent Republic of Iceland is founded on 17th June.
1946	At the end of the war, the Americans ask for approval for several military bases, but their request is rejected by the Icelandic Alþing.
1949	Iceland becomes a founder member of the United Nations but the decision to keep an American-dominated NATO military base on the island is not popular with the population.
1952	Iceland's national waters are extended to four miles.
1958	Iceland's national waters are extended to 12 miles prompting the first 'Cod War' with Britain when British navy ships escort British trawlers into the new boundaries.

1963	A violent offshore volcanic eruption gives birth to the island of Surtsey.
1965	Denmark agrees to return originals of the *Icelandic Sagas* that had been taken to Copenhagen.
1971	The first manuscripts arrive from Denmark to scenes of jubilation at Reykjavik quayside.
1972	Iceland's national waters are extended to 80.5km, resulting in the second Cod War.
1973	The eruption of the island of Heimaey prompts an evacuation of the population and intervention to save the harbour. Nixon and Pompidou hold a summit in Reykjavik.
1974	1100 years of inhabitation celebrations. The A1 ring road is completed.
1975	Iceland unilaterally increases its territorial waters to 200 miles, bringing it again into conflict with the British in a third Cod War.
1980	First woman President, Vigdís Finnbogadóttir is elected.
1982	The International Whaling Commission (a group of whale hunting nations) calls a moratorium on all hunting to study depleting whale numbers.
1986	Reagan – Gorbachev summit in Reykjavik marks the beginning of the end of the Communist era.
1994	Iceland concludes an agreement with the EU giving it access to the European internal market.
1995	A winter of avalanches kills 34 people in the Westfjords.
2001	Iceland is accepted into the Schengen Agreement.
2003	The Icelandic parliament approves the resumption of whaling for research purposes with over 20 animals taken during July and August. The plan for the Kárahnjúkár Dam (*see pp111*) is also approved.
2005	Iceland offers controversial American chess player Bobby Fischer political asylum despite the opposition of the US government.

The Vikings

'... on the 7th of the Ides of January, the havoc of heathen men miserably destroyed God's church at Lindisfarne, through rapine and slaughter.'
THE ANGLO-SAXON CHRONICLE, UK

Until very recently this was the popular view of the Vikings: savage, pagan brutes who would appear on the horizon in their boats, land and make a lightning raid, rape and pillage, and then depart as quickly as they came, carrying slaves in tow. *The Anglo-Saxon Chronicle is* one of several accounts of Viking activities during the late first millennium and it has coloured our view of these mysterious men of the north. Over the last 20 years, however, new archaeological research has changed our impression of the Vikings. They are now viewed as traders rather than raiders, and sophisticates rather than savages.

There was never a single united Viking culture – they would have described themselves as Danes, Swedes or Norwegians – but one thing they did have in common was their language – Old Norse.

The Vikings headed west to northern UK, to Iceland, Greenland, Baffin Island and, it is thought, North America. They ventured south into what is now Normandy in France, and they also travelled east through the Caspian and Black Seas, reaching Constantinople and beyond. They may have raided, but then they also traded and settled; especially in the lands of northwestern Europe.

Who were the Vikings?

The term 'Viking' is used by scholars to describe the peoples who travelled out of their homeland in Scandinavia to dominate Europe from c.800–1100.

The Viking Ship

The secret of the success of the Viking diaspora was their shipbuilding ability. The crafts they built were the jets of their day. The *drekar*, popularly known

as the 'Viking longship', was a dual power vessel with sails and oars. It was 'clinker built' (with wooden planks overlapping downward, held in place by clinched nails), making it lightweight and flexible, and with a rudder rather than a keel giving the boat a very shallow draft for entering shallow waters.

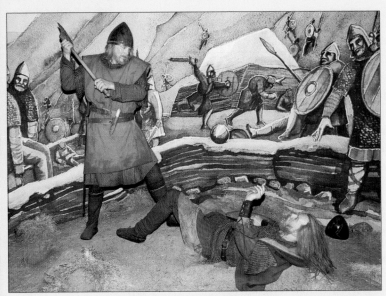

A *drekar* found at Roskilde Fjord in Denmark was 47m long with 72 oars, a 200sq m sail and a draft of only 1m. It could carry a crew of one hundred.

Viking Lifestyles

The Vikings were consummate farmers and traders. They lived in village settlements or farmsteads. The long winters were spent on making handicrafts, which were traded in towns in the summer. While the men were away on trade missions the women would assume full responsibility for all aspects of daily life; but, in general, the responsibilities of men were hunting and fishing while women ran the house, and undertook weaving, spinning and sail-making.

The Viking Runes

The Viking runes were an important part of Viking society. They were a set of mystical symbols used to cast spells and reveal the future. The Vikings believed that the runes were revealed to their god Odin (*see pp70–71*) and thus they were imbued with sacred power that could be harnessed for good and evil. Rune masters who could cast and interpret the sacred messages were highly respected by the community.

Later, the runes were used as an alphabet of phonetic sounds that could be put together to form coherent sentences.

Facing page: Ingólfur Arnarson
Above: Viking axeman

Governance

The fierce self-determination and independence of Icelanders come through most clearly in their attitude to politics. You will find very few statues raised to commemorate the leaders and a jovial cynicism about domestic and international statesmen. Yet, there is a passion for social issues and about where Iceland is heading in the future that show a keen approval of the political process.

The Icelandic flag

The Alþing
Most early settlers fled to Iceland to escape the regime of the Norwegian monarchy, and in particular the tyranny of Harald the Fairhead whose heavy hand stretched across Scandinavia and into Scotland and Ireland. The early Icelandic population was therefore vehemently egalitarian, anti-monarchy and eschewed rule by any kind of force. However, as the population grew, it became clear that some kind of governing body would be needed to adjudicate in disputes over land and social justice. They solved this problem with a revolutionary new system of government – the Alþing, the world's first parliament.

Founded in AD 930, the Alþing was basically an annual meeting where problems were discussed and resolved, and rules decided by mutual consent. Lawmaking and debate took place at the Lögberg or 'Law Rock', an outcrop at a site northeast of Reykjavik. Here the presiding official elected for the session, the Lögsöumaður or Law Maker, would chair meetings and publicly proclaim

any decisions made or laws passed. The meetings were open to all free men but decisions were made by the legislature or Lögrétta, which comprised a number of goðar or local leaders plus the Lögsöumaður. Later, as the system developed, a judiciary was established with the fimmtardómur of 48 judges appointed by the Lögrétta. In its heyday the annual Alþing was a major social event and a huge fair would accompany the serious business. A large encampment or búðir was set up to accommodate the crowds.

However, with the arrival of Danish rule the Alþing became a shadow of its former self, acting simply as an enforcement agency of laws enacted by the monarchy in Copenhagen and imposed on the Icelandic people.

The Independence Movement
Jón Sigurðsson (1811–1879) is regarded as the father of Icelandic nationalism. The Republic of Iceland was founded on his birthday and it is celebrated as National Day, although he can by no means be described as a freedom fighter

in the same mould as, say, Che Guevara. Born in the remote Westfjords, he moved to Copenhagen in 1833 to continue his studies and then went to work in the repository where the originals of the great *Icelandic sagas* were stored.

Being so close to the 'soul of Iceland' captured his imagination and he began his campaign for Icelandic self-determination. He became the voice of Iceland in Denmark and through carefully phrased verbal argument and a diplomatic approach gradually made his mark with the Danish authorities.

In 1845, by decree of the Danish Government, the Icelandic Alþing was reinstated as a legislative body. Suffrage was limited to males over 25 and of independent means – so it was not exactly democratic; its head was Jón Sigurðsson. Though it did initiate legislation on a number of domestic matters, it was still, in essence, an advisory body to the government in Copenhagen.

In 1874 a new Danish constitution granted the Alþing sovereignty over Iceland's internal issues, though the crown still had the right to veto legislation and often did where it thought the change would conflict with Danish national interest. This was Jón's final triumph as he died five years later.

The momentum carried the process on after his death. In 1903 Iceland was granted home rule and a parliament of 40 members was elected by proportional

The British Governor's residence

The Alþing in Reykjavik

Iceland Today

The Alþing currently has 63 members with nine members elected from each of the island's six constituencies and the remaining members chosen according to proportional representation to reflect their party's popularity. The minimum percentage of vote that a party must receive to be eligible for extra proportional seats is five.

General elections take place once every four years, with every citizen over 18 and living in Iceland being eligible to vote. Electoral participation is high; 87 per cent of voters turned out in 2003.

The Iceland's President is elected by popular vote every four years. The current incumbent, Olafur Ragnar Grimsson, has been in office since 1996. The Prime Minister is appointed by the President and the post is currently held by Halldór Ásgrímsson (since 2004).

Parliamentary sessions open on 1st October every year. The first order of business is to elect a President of the Alþing for that session. He or she ensures that the debates and procedure proceed within the rules, and that all opinions are heard. The Alþing sessions are open to the public.

Members also take on other roles, including participating in the 12 standing advisory committees, and in international delegations such as those

representation. An Icelandic minister was responsible to the parliament and acted as liaison with Copenhagen. Just after the First World War, on December 1st 1918, Iceland became a sovereign state in union with its former colonial master and the Alþing became a national legislative chamber. In 1944, Iceland declared itself an independent parliamentary democracy with a single legislative chamber, the Alþing.

to the Nordic Council or to liaison with the EU.

Party Politics
Currently the Alþing power game revolves around five parties (listed here in alphabetical order):
The Alliance Party (Samfylkingin) – a centre-left social democratic mainstream party.
The Independence Party (Sjálfstæðisflokkurinn) – a right wing party with a desire to decrease governmental intervention.
The Leftist Green Party (Vinstrihreyfingin-Grænt Framboð) – a party covering the far left, pro-environment and anti-NATO concerns and feminists.
The Liberal Party (Frjálslyndir) – a rightwing party with a desire to protect Iceland's traditional rights (with particular concerns for fishing and whaling).
The Progressive Party (Framsónarflokkurinn) – a party with a centre-right stance, in favour of few economic regulations and reduced governmental interference.

The future
The big debate over the next few years will be whether Iceland will join the EU. Potential problems include what happens to the all-important Icelandic fishing rights because Europe is cutting quotas throughout the community. However, Iceland feels European in its greater cultural and economic partnerships, and some think it is only a matter of time before the island joins the fold.

Signboard for Konungsrikið Ísland

An enamelled badge

Culture

Art isn't put on a pedestal [in Iceland]. It's part of life – like baking a cake.
BJÖRK
Seventeen Magazine August 1997

A sculpture at Borgarnes

Pop diva Björk's quote above sums up the Icelander's approach to the arts. There are very few countries in the world where artistic endeavour is so closely entwined with everyday life, or where art in all its forms is so accessible and understood by ordinary people. Icelanders are comfortable with creativity and this is tied directly to a rich vein of oral and written culture passed down through generations.

As you travel around, you will find that almost every town in Iceland remembers a local hero with a plaque, a statue or a small museum. Invariably those revered are writers or artists, in stark contrast to the generals and politicians who tend to be honoured in the rest of Europe.

That said, it took many generations for culture and the arts to become a 'profession'. 'Jobbing' artists who wrote

The Akureyri Art Museum

or painted in between making a living as postmaster, sheriff or farmer were the norm until the late 18th century. Even today many young musicians play for pleasure rather than in the hope of fame, and may delve into several forms of the art rather than specialising in one as is the norm in most societies.

The Legacy of the Sagas

The influence that the medieval *Sagas* (*see pp28–9*) still have on the cultural life of modern Iceland cannot be overstated. The *Sagas* were written centuries ago but the Icelandic language has changed little since that time and the stories are still read in their original form by today's population – something that the English cannot do with their literary heroes: Chaucer's *Canterbury Tales* or Shakespeare's epic plays. The *Sagas'* recurring themes of the details of everyday life combined with epic trials of human fortitude are picked up by modern writers, painters and filmmakers. The mythology of the stories has been infused into the bedrock of the Icelandic belief system, and it finds an outlet in the creativity of passing generations.

Words

Iceland's modern literary giant is Halldór Kiljan Laxness, who was awarded the Nobel Prize for Literature in 1955 – the first person to achieve international fame while writing in his native Icelandic. Born Halldór Helgason, he spent his childhood in the countryside before leaving Iceland to explore the outside world. He converted to Catholicism during a sojourn in

France, adopting the name Laxness and the middle name Kiljan after the Irish saint – this became his *nom de plume.* During this era he also wrote his first major novel, *The Great Weaver of Kashmir.* Soon afterwards he discovered socialism and left religion behind.

A prolific writer with over 60 major works, Laxness wrote his seminal series of books during the 1930s after returning to Iceland. His novels have a central theme: seen through the eyes of the disenfranchised hero or heroine, the beautifully woven narrative features the recurring problems of poverty, exploitation and an unsympathetic establishment.

The original manuscript of the *Sagas*

Carrying on in this literary vein are young novelists such as Vigdis Grímsdóttir, Ólafur Gunnarsson, Guðbergur Bergsson and Hallgrimur Helgason (b.1959). Hegalson's book, *101 Reykjavik*, was turned into a successful film. In many ways, he encapsulates the Icelander's approach to the arts. He is a recognised artist, a stand-up comedian, a cartoonist and playwright, and sees nothing unusual in this multi-genre approach.

Painting and Sculpture

Visit any of the turf and wood farmsteads around the island and it soon becomes clear how adept the Icelanders were and are at carving decoration into wood, bone and horn. This was almost exclusively a cottage industry and there were no fulltime artists and no opportunities to study art without moving abroad. Ásgrímur Jónsson (1876-1958) broke the mould when he became Iceland's first professional artist and as the 20th century saw the flowering of modernism, Icelanders embraced the new movements with relish. Jóhannes Sveinsson Kjarval (1885–1972) was

Ásgrímur's main peer. His Bohemian lifestyle saw him remain poor throughout the whole of his career despite being feted during his lifetime. His eccentric approach to life meant he sometimes had to give away or barter his paintings in return for food and shelter.

The same period also saw the birth of sculpture in Iceland and its two earliest exponents are still highly revered. Einar Jónsson (1874–1954) trained in Copenhagen and Rome but returned to his homeland for long periods. He worked mostly in plaster but since his death, several of his major works have been recast in bronze. Ásmundur Sveinsson (1893–1982) was a couple of decades younger the Einar. He studied in Sweden and was heavily influenced by the arrival of Bauhaus.

Later, Sigurjón Ólafson (1908–82) completes a trio of talent. An experimental artist originally trained as a house painter, he has 18 monumental pieces on display in the capital. All these three artists have museums or galleries dedicated to them in Reykjavik where major works, along with personal effects and workspaces, allow us to delve into their rationale and motivation.

Today, the visual arts world is vibrant with new genres of photography and electronic media broadening the palate. Erró, born Goðmundur Goðmundersson in 1932, is a leading modern pop art virtuoso who has donated a number of works to the Reykjavik Art Museum, though he has lived outside Iceland for many years. Orn Þosteinsson

Road sign

The President's summer residence

and Steimunn Thórurinsdóttir are both successful full-time sculptors, while Rafn Sigurbjörnsson is a leading landscape photographer. A visit to the various buildings that comprise the Reykyavik City Art Museum (*see p45*) will give you an insight to their work.

Theatre

Despite its small population, Iceland supports two professional theatre companies and both perform works written by native playwrights including Sigurður Pálsson, Bjarni Jónsson, Ólafur Haukur Símonarson, Þorunn Sigurðardóttir and Sveinn Einarsson.

Art for all
You can rent art by the month for up to three years from Reykjavik City Library in their Artótek. There are over 900 pieces to choose from.

Major novels by writers such as Laxness have also been transformed into stage plays since the 1990s. Iceland's theatre is probably the most difficult area of the arts for non-Icelandic speakers to access, because of the language barrier.

The worlds of theatre and film (*see p27*) are merging more and more with many writers, directors and actors actively working in both genres.

Music

Since the start of the 1980s, Iceland has been a hot spot in the world of popular music, led by, but by no means limited to, the unique musical phenomenon that is Björk.

Björk released her first album in 1976 at the age of 11 and only a few years later took to punk like a duck to water. The band she fronted, the *Sugarcubes*, exploded onto the international scene in

Iceland at the Multiplex
Iceland can be spotted in the following blockbuster Hollywood movies: James Bond's *Die Another Day*, *Tomb Raider*, *Batman Begins* and the upcoming Clint Eastwood-directed *Flags of Our Fathers*. The Icelandic authorities offer tax breaks to companies filming here, and this boosts the economy by millions of dollars, brings extra employment to the island and does a great job for the Iceland Tourist Board by promoting the fantastic natural locations.

the late 1980s. Later she embarked upon a successful solo career but throughout has retained her inimitable and indefinable perspective on music and the world.

But this writer/musician/performer did not emerge from a musical vacuum. A generation of young Icelandic musicians had laid the bedrock of today's vibrant scene, creating a network of interconnecting bands with a reputation for expanding the envelope. Eschewing completely the 'manufactured boy band/bland cover version' approach, they wrote their own compositions and played their own instruments – often fitting in seasons as artists, actors or filmmakers. The Icelandic cultural scene certainly is not about being pigeonholed.

The momentum continues into the new millennium with bands like Sigur Rós, Singapore Sling or Cat Power, who, while not emulating Björk's success in terms of wealth and

record sales, certainly carry forward the torch of Icelandic tradition to the international stage.

Film

There was no film industry in Iceland until the late 1980s, but in a few years since then a small band of directors and their often inexperienced cast and crew have taken the world of cinema by storm. The founding father of the industry is Fridrik Thór Fridriksson whose energies led to the founding of the Icelandic Film Corporation in 1987; the same year, the government approved the creation of the Cinema Foundation. Icelandic film made it into the big time when the Fridriksson-directed *Children of Nature* was nominated for an Oscar in the best foreign film category in 1991 and it has been on a roll ever since.

Today the domestic film industry produces around seven films a year. Themes lean heavily towards pseudo-documentary, telling the story of fettered and frustrated youth in a socially fragmented modern society. Some of the best include *101 Reykjavik* by Baltasar Kormákur (2000), *Noi Albinoi* by Dagur Kári (2002) and Ágúst Godmundsson's *The Seagull's Laughter* (2001). Fridriksson himself has gone on to make more films including *Angels of the Universe* in 2000 and *Cold Fever*, released in 2005.

A statue from the period of Danish rule

Tourists in downtown Reykjavik

The Icelandic Eddas and Sagas

The single most important source of information about Iceland's history and the central element of Iceland's national psyche, the *Sagas* are a unique series of epic accounts relating the history of the original Viking settlers penned by later Christian chroniclers directly from an earlier oral tradition.

Over 40 *Sagas* were written. They give us a blow-by-blow account of Icelandic society from its first fledgling agreements through to the collapse of the rule of law. They are also filled with wonderfully intimate details of love affairs, family feuds, births and deaths as the generations passed. They are not just dry records but rich chronicles of daily life.

Most of the *Sagas* were written anonymously but the younger *Edda and Heimskringla* – a book about the lives of the Norwegian monarchy – was written by Snorri Sturluson, a celebrated writer in his own time.

The Eddas

Eddas differ from the *Sagas* in that they relate to the Norse mythology with epic tales of the old pagan gods (*see pp70–71*). Though the *Sagas* do contain a mythological element they deal mainly with human relations.

Why were they written?

Saga specialist Arni Björnsson feels that the answer lies in the unique structure of early Icelandic society. With no monarchy and no hereditary aristocracy, the most important people in society were independent farmers, rich and poor. Perhaps these farmers wanted to preserve their history as a way of celebrating their success in building a new nation.

The *Sagas* Today

Today, many historians view the *Sagas* as important historical texts, although they recognise that they contain romanticised

Facing page: *Sagas* chroniclers
This page left: Snorri Sturluson;
right: *Sagas* text

elements. Archaeologists found traces of a settlement at L'Anse aux Meadows in Newfoundland that is believed to be of Viking origin by studying *Saga* texts. The *Sagas* feature in the curriculum of all primary schools in Iceland so everyone has knowledge of the first settlers/heroes almost from day one and they are still bestsellers in their native land.

Snorri Sturluson

The life of the most famous *Saga* writer, Snorri, reads like a *Saga* itself. Born in Hvamm in western Iceland in 1179 into an influential landowning family, he followed in his father's footsteps and became a goðar or local leader with many tracts of land. In 1215 he was elected as *Lögsöumaður* (*see p18*) and a couple of years later he travelled to

Norway to meet King Hakon Hakonarson, for whom he wrote an epic poem.

Snorri lived in a time, now known as the Sturlung Age, when Icelandic society was imploding. The writer and his family were in the thick of the action. Snorri fell from royal approval and a rival nephew became the king's favourite. When things got ugly Snorri went into exile in Norway, but when his nephew was killed he thought it safe to return to Iceland despite a royal decree banning him. King Hakon decreed that Snorri return to Norway or face death but Hakon's agent in Iceland, Gisor Thorvaldsson, who was building a power base for himself, did not offer him an option. On September 23rd 1241, a gang of men arrived at Snorri's farm and he was brutally killed.

Festivals and Events

Iceland has a whole host of festivals, many going back to its Viking and pagan ancestry but some remarkably modern and 21st-century ones. The arts scene is very busy in the short summer season when almost every gallery or venue has a special event on the calendar.

All-night parties in June

Icelanders enjoy letting their hair down and it has to be said that national celebrations usually involve imbibing large amounts of alcohol. However, the high spirits rarely spill over into drunken behaviour. These people somehow know how to keep their balance.

January
Þrettándinn the 13th day after Christmas, marking the end of Iceland's festive season, is celebrated with bonfires, fireworks and traditional songs (6th).
Bóndadagur – marking the beginning of the Thorri Viking festival that lasts through February, has traditional festive dances, singing and food (23rd).

February
Konudagur marks the beginning of Góa in the old Icelandic calendar (22nd).

February–March
Buns Day – the Monday before Ash Wednesday is celebrated with the consumption of cream puffs.
Bursting Day – the Tuesday before Ash Wednesday has Icelanders eating salted meat and peas until they 'burst'.
Ash Wednesday – On the seventh Wednesday before Easter, children dress in costumes and tour the towns singing in return for sweets.

April
The First Day of Summer is a day of festivities with parades and other activities – remember that these people emerge on this day from a winter of almost total darkness (around 20th).

Late May–early June
Reykjavik Arts Festival – a gathering of native artists to showcase their work.

June
Iceland's longest days are celebrated with all night parties, walks and hikes.
Seaman's Day has cultural events, parades and other activities with the sea and sailors being the theme (1st weekend).
National Day witnesses parades and parties all around the country (17th).
Icelandic Open – a golf tournament that invites its competitors to tee off under the light of the midnight sun (end-June).

Late June–early July
Icelandair Horse Fair brings the equine community together.

July
Akureyri Arts Festival is celebrated

with plays, concerts and exhibitions all over the city (all month–end-August).
Light Nights English Theatre season (mid-July–late-August).
The summer concert season, Skálholt cathedral complex (mid-July–mid August).

August
Bank Holiday Weekend – various events and festivities mark the national holiday and long weekend.
Gay Pride sees a day of parades and open-air concerts (early August).
Reykjavik Marathon – the city gives itself over to serious and fun runners.

An average of 3,500 people take part, including around 500 foreign competitors (mid-August).
Reykjavik Culture Night – half a million people flock to the city for hours of free concerts and other activities (3rd weekend)(*see p157*).
Festival of Sacred Arts, Hallgrímskirkja – classical musical performances by international artists, choirs and orchestras (late August, bienniaally on odd years).

September
Réttir – all the sheep and horses that have been free-grazing around the island are rounded up.

The Reykjavik Marathon, about to begin

Troll with a Viking Helmet

Impressions

Iceland is Europe's northwesternmost country, set just below the Arctic Circle and surrounded by the cold waters of the Atlantic Ocean. It is the most sparsely populated country on the continent and its wide open spaces can be reached by a three-hour flight from mainland Europe or in just over five hours from northeastern US.

When to go

More than most other destinations on the planet it is important to pick the right season to visit to get the most out of Iceland.

The 'Land of the Midnight Sun', has days of widely differing lengths, with long days in summer and short, almost totally dark days in winter.

The year round sunrise and sunset times in Reykjavik are given below – in towns further north, days are longer in summer and shorter in winter.

The 21-hour summer days and 5-hour winter days make a big seasonal difference to the atmosphere of the island. Summer is packed with festivals and events, fun runs and sporting contests, and there is a very jovial atmosphere. Locals are outdoors walking and hiking in the national parks and in the highlands, camping, fishing and getting back to their roots.

The 'tourist' season is remarkably short – crammed into seven or eight weeks in July and early August – and this is not only because the days are longest at this time. It is also because vacationing university and high school students are free to take up the slack as hotel waiters, hotel room cleaners, museum or outdoor pursuits guides. Summer is also the safest and surest time to visit Iceland's hinterland. The roads are open (usually from late May to mid-September depending on weather conditions) and in the best condition.

All this does not mean that you should not visit outside this short period. Iceland has much to offer in every season, especially if you have specialist interests. The island benefits from the warm currents of the Gulf Stream that forces warm air northward tempering the fiercest Arctic temperatures. The weather can be clement through spring and autumn and on a sunny winter's day the island looks magical though the interior is off-limits to all but specialist vehicles.

Date	Sunrise	Sunset
January 1	11.19	15.45
February 1	10.07	17.16
March 1	08.35	18.47
April 1	06.45	20.20
May 1	04.59	21.52
June 1	03.22	23.31
July 1	03.05	23.57
August 1	04.34	22.31
September 1	06.10	20.43
October 1	07.36	18.57
November 1	09.11	17.11
December 1	10.46	15.48

Many of Iceland's major attractions are accessible throughout the year – they don't turn off the Strokkur geyser in September – and some of its activities, including Quad biking, are better when there is snow on the ground. The island's fledgling ski industry has facilities for the sport under floodlight, so even when the daylight is short, the time on the piste is longer than that in, say, the Alps, Dolomites or Pyrenees.

Reykjavik is a year-round destination and looks particularly beautiful with a covering of snow on a crisp winter's day. The city's residents are used to the cold and dark, and the weekly pub-crawl carries on whatever the weather conditions.

What to wear

There is a motto in Iceland: if you don't like the weather wait for five minutes because it is bound to change. Many visitors have experienced four seasons in one day.

Iceland's weather can and does change frequently. You can get cold spells in summer and rain at all times of the year.

So the motto is 'be prepared', and carry warm and waterproof clothing no matter what time of year you travel. A layering system is advisable so that if you feel warm you can take off a layer of clothing and vice versa. Breathable lightweight fabrics are ideal for the climate, and microfibre fleeces that add little weight to your luggage but provide good insulation.

A cyclist planning his route

Tourists board a sightseeing coach

A good weatherproof jacket is a must along with comfortable shoes for city walking and rugged shoes for the rest of the country – remember that the lava flows and predominance of volcanic rock can wreak havoc on shoe-soles, and the uneven surfaces on the hills and coastline mean that you need good ankle support.

If you are travelling in a rental car, carry warm clothing with you in case of emergency.

Getting Around

The last 30 years have seen tremendous development in transport links. The main ring road around the island was completed in 1974, allowing easy access for the first time to the northeast region across the sandur volcanic desert. Since then the asphalting of roads has continued apace. The huge progress in motor vehicle technology over the last 20 or so years has made a big difference to getting around. Four-wheel drive, power steering and ABS have made driving safer for self-driven vehicles, buses and tour vehicles, which now come fitted with standard air conditioning.

Driving yourself is the only way to get to Iceland's remote attractions – its farthest fjords and most spectacular mountains. A car allows you flexibility and independence. But it is still possible to enjoy a cross-section of what the country has to offer without a car. You can take one of the many day or multiple-day tours organised by Reykjavik Excursions or Iceland Excursions. These have been specifically designed to showcase the best of Iceland's landscape and culture.

Or, there are cross-country buses that link all the major towns. Contact *www.dice.is* for details of multi-destination passes. In summer buses even run over the highland road through the heart of the country. However, journey times may be long and connections are not always seamlessly planned.

The other option is to take an internal flight. Planes from the airport in the heart of Reykjavik (for more details see *www.airiceland.is*) fly to a range of Icelandic towns (most internal flights last less than an hour), and you can pick up a rental car or get on to a tour bus once you have reached your destination.

Culture Shock

The following thoughts are a truly non-scientific listing of the idiosyncrasies of Iceland. They are in no particular order but simply offer a flavour of the national psyche.

Irreverence

Icelanders have a mischievous and sarcastic sense of humour and a forthright approach once you have broken the ice with them. They hold little truck with power or authority. Expect to be surprised by the way conversations turn deep and meaningful within minutes of your meeting an Icelander.

Land of the Midnight Sun?

We have already mentioned that Iceland is the land of the midnight sun and its citizens, especially those living in Reykjavik, make the most of the long days by camping, hiking, 'hotpotting' and holding raucous midnight parties. But, conversely, it is also the land of the lunchtime moon and research has proved that long periods of darkness can contribute to a problem called

Enjoying the midday sun at a cafe in Reykjavik

Walking along the beach near Reykjavik

'seasonal affective disorder', or, in the form of the most appropriate acronym, SAD. It is difficult to maintain one's equilibrium in winter and a percentage of the population does suffer from depression. For some, heavy drinking is the way to get through the winter despite the high price of alcohol.

Trolls

In a recent survey, most Icelanders said they believed in trolls. These naughty little rascals wreak havoc across the island causing cars to break down, plumbing to go haywire and traffic to snarl-up just when you want to catch

that transport connection. Some Icelanders think the trolls were stowaways aboard Viking ships during the very first days of settlement; and that they loved this remote landscape so much that they inhabited all the little nooks and crannies on the coast and in the hills. Your best bet to avoid their effect on your trip is to think happy Zen thoughts as the creatures are believed to thrive on negativity!

What's in a Name?

Icelanders have worked for centuries on a patronymic name system. There are no family names but the name trail shows the lineage of each family through the generations. Children take a given first name, then the father's first name followed by either 'sson' (meaning son of) or 'sdottir' (meaning 'daughter of'). When women marry they don't take their husband's name. So a family of four – father, mother, son and daughter – will all have different last names.

As an example, if Sigrun and Jón have a girl and a boy called Döra and Árnar, the little girl will be known as Döra Jónsdottir while the little boy will be called Árnar Jónsson. When Árnar grows up to have his own son called Leifur, the child will be known as Leifur Árnarsson.

Because of this unique system, Icelanders have never developed a formal approach to social interaction. People call each other by their first names no matter what their social relations. The only people to have formal titles are the President and the Bishop of Iceland (and even then the

President is referred to as 'the President of Iceland Ólafur Ragnar Grímsson', not as 'President Grímsson'). The egalitarian first-names-only approach of Icelanders is exceptionally refreshing.

Take a look in an Icelandic phone directory and you will find people are listed by their given names!

A Sticky Situation

Where other countries may have the scourge of other kinds of litter on the streets, Iceland's menace is chewing gum left in strategic places such as under café tables or public benches, and always on the major pedestrian thoroughfares. In cooler weather and in winter the gum hardens and causes a few problems but on a wonderfully warm summer day the only problem could be that you find yourself firmly attached to your temporary seat!

A Fantastic Set of Wheels

Without doubt, one of the most exciting and interesting parts of your visit to Iceland will be the driving. Away from the main asphalted roads are hundreds of kilometres of compacted dirt roads that make you feel like you are on some kind of a pioneering expedition. And after a couple of days on the road, you will notice that you are developing a whole new mind-set as far as motor vehicles are concerned.

You will start by noticing a little twinge of envy for the guy in the truck sporting super-sized tyres that passes

A traditional family tea at home

you on the road. You will find yourself stopping in the street to admire little accessories on the exterior like roof spotlights and tow hooks. The longer you are on the island, the more alluring the big Arctic trucks, with the ultimate in off-road modifications, will become. Call it some kind of hypnotic effect – or maybe it is the strong landscape – that brings out the macho rally driver in all of us.

Mind the Doors
In many hotel rooms doors open out into the corridor rather than into the room. Beware of this as you exit every morning, and if walking down hotel corridors, don't get too close to the doors.

A Lingering Aftertaste
Icelanders have been brought up on the adage that a dose of cod liver oil (lýsi) a

Enjoying a quiet moment

day will keep you fit and healthy, and it is certainly true that the vitamin D in the oil compensates for what they don't get from sunlight during the winter.

Being generous folk, they also put out a bottle of the oil at the breakfast table in hotels and guesthouses so that you too can take a tot every morning. It is wise to remember though that this cod liver oil is not the type sanitised for the rest of the world. Iceland's cod liver oil smells and tastes fishy.

Prices
There is no doubt that prices in Iceland will make you wince. That is all that needs to be said.

Boarding schools
If you were wondering about schooling, children from remote farmsteads are used to leaving home for boarding school during term-time. This is another reason why Icelanders are confident and self-reliant – because they leave the nest so early. Most schools are so modern and comfortable that they double-up as hotels during the summer holidays.

Hunting and whaling
Icelanders have made a living from commercial whaling for centuries, and hunting has supplemented their meagre diet in this harsh environment. Today, the attitudes towards both activities may have changed around the world but many Icelanders still regard them as legitimate. This is one country where you will be able to hear a coherent and structured argument in favour of whaling and hunting.

An outdoor café on the Húsavík harbour front

Reykjavik

Reykjavik is a place full of surprises and contradictions. A capital city, yet not much bigger than a large town. A city remote from the world, yet right at the heart of it with the help of modern technology. A city with an unfriendly climate, yet known to be one of the party capitals of the world. A city where everyone is into creativity. This is a seriously 'happening' place, yet it takes it all in its stride.

Cafe in Reykjavik

Reykjavik has lots to offer all the year round. It is a friendly city where you can walk between attractions, and cultural tourism can be interspersed with a coffee or something stronger at one of numerous atmospheric café bars where you can rest weary feet. As day turns into night the bars and clubs – from techno to hard rock – come into their own, especially at weekends, as an army of revellers stroll from establishment to establishment. The *runtur*, as it is known, has become legendary in the clubbing world.

Fjölskyldu – og húsdýragarðurinn (Reykjavik Zoo and Family Park)

At the heart of the park is Reykjavik Zoo, with the only live animal collection on the island. Don't expect to see any exotic species as most would not be very happy in Iceland's climate. Instead, this

Reykjavik

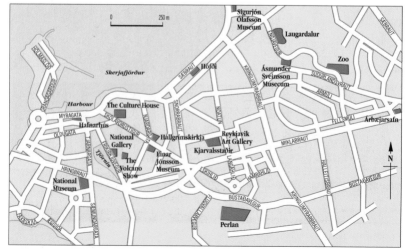

A flea market in Reykjavik

is the perfect place to find native species, many of which can rarely be seen in the wild because they inhabit the most remote corners of the island. You will find Arctic foxes and reindeer here, as well as domestic species such as horses and cattle, plus the sheep that are too skittish to approach in the wild. There is a marine area with seals and North Atlantic fish species – the kind of thing you will probably be eating for dinner!

When the children tire of the animals there is a play area with climbing frames, towers and other fun stuff.
Bus routes 2, 14 and 15. Laugardalur (see p42), 104 Reykjavik.
Tel: 553 7870. www.mu.is.
Open: May 15–Aug 22 daily 10am–6pm;

Aug 23–May 14 daily 10am–5pm.
Admission charge.

Hafn (Reykjavik Harbour)
The capital still has a fishing fleet and there is an air of gritty workaday reality at the port where the catch of the day is landed, frozen and dispatched in a remarkably short time. Come down to the harbour to take advantage of the whale or puffin-watching trips that depart daily (weather permitting) and trips out to Viðey (*p53*).

Hallgrímskirkja (Hallgríms Church)
The towering stark white outline of Iceland's largest place of worship can be seen from all around the surrounding countryside. Inaugurated in 1974, its rather dour though expansive façade is designed to resemble one of Iceland's most evocative landscapes, the sheer face of a glacier or ice flow. Unusually, the church was named after a clergyman, Reverend Hallgrímur Pétursson, who wrote some of Iceland's finest hymns. The interior of the cathedral is uninspiring but a trip to the top of the 75m steeple is a must for the fantastic views across the city.

Reykjavik Tourist Card
The Reykjavik Tourist Card offers entrance to a number of museums and attractions including the thermal pools in the city, along with free public transport and 30 minutes' Internet access at the Tourist Office. There are also discounts on some tours.
Cards are valid for 24, 48 or 72 hours, and can be bought from tourist information offices and some hotels. For more information visit the city website (*www.visitreykjavik.is*).

Hallgríms Church

In the square in front of the church is a magnificent heroic statue of Leifur Eiríksson, the discover of Vinland (now thought to be North America). It was presented to the Icelandic people by the USA to mark the 1000-year anniversary of the founding of the Alþing.
Skólavörðuholti, 101 Reykjavik. Tel: 510 1000. www.hallgrimskirkja.is Open: daily 9am–5pm. Tower open: 9am–4.45pm. Admission charge for tower.

Höfði

Set overlooking the Reykjavik shoreline, this early 1900s catalogue house ordered from Norway from the French consul has a rather spectacular history. During the Second World War, Winston Churchill and Marlene Dietreich both stayed here (though, I hasten to add, not together) and it became seat of British diplomacy after the war. The British Ambassador swore the house was haunted and it was sold. It later came into the hands of the municipality of Reykjavik who used it as a reception venue. It has seen presidents, queens and other heads of state but its finest moment was in 1986 when it hosted the historic Reagan – Gorbachev summit that saw the beginning of the end of the Cold War.
Borgartún. Closed to public.

Laugardalur

The largest green space in the city is a magnet for families in the long summer evenings and sunny weekends throughout the year. The city zoo (*see pp40–41*) is the major attraction here but you can spend time enjoying other activities as well. The Botanical Gardens covering 2.5 hectares house over 5,000 plant species, and include a woodland garden, rhododendrons (best in May) and a greenhouse containing 130 foreign species. The most recent area, planted in 2000, displays Icelandic plants of economic value with culinary and medicinal herbs.

Close by, the Laugardalur Thermal and Swimming Pool (*see p146*) is the biggest in the city and features hotpots and an Olympic-sized pool.
Botanical Gardens. Skúlatún 2, 105 Reykjavik. Tel: 553 8870. Open: Apr–Sept daily 10am–10pm; Oct–Mar daily 10am–5pm. Admission free.

Listasafn Íslands (National Gallery of Iceland)

The National Gallery's collection comprises leading Icelandic art of the 19th and 20th centuries. Showcasing key works from each genre and artist and maintaining a huge reference library, it is the island's most important repository of art.

Statue of Leifur Eiríksson

An overview of the city

When it was founded in 1885 the collection mainly comprised pieces by Danish artists. It was not until 1902 that the first piece by an Icelandic artist – *Outlaws* by Einar Jónsson – was added to the catalogue. Today the gallery houses over 10,000 works. Paintings were displayed in the Alþing (Parliament) building until 1950 and finally installed in this permanent home – an old freezing plant built in 1916 – in 1987.

The gallery offers a strong programme of temporary exhibitions often charting artistic genres or the development of art through certain periods. The small international collection features works by Picasso and Munch.

Bus routes 1, 3, 4, 5, 6, 11, 12, 13 and 14.
Fríkirkjuvegur 7, 101 Reykjavik.
Tel: 515 9600. Open: Tue–Sun
11am–5pm. Admission charge.

Minjasafn Einar Jónsson (Einar Jónsson Museum)

This rather unassuming building hidden behind trees on Cathedral Square was in fact Iceland's first art gallery when it opened in 1923. Designed by sculptor Einar Jónsson in the Art Nouveau style that was so fashionable at the time, the museum displays over 300 of his sculptures and paintings spanning a career of 60 years – from the earliest mythology-inspired pieces to the later more figurative works including the evocative *The Pioneer* of 1911 and the heroic *Protection* finished in 1934. The garden contains 26 bronze castings of Einar's works.

Eiriksgata, 101 Reykjavik. Tel: 551 3797.
www.skulptur.is. Open: Jun–15 Sept
Tue–Sun 2–5pm; Sept 16–May Sat–Sun
2–5pm. Closed: Dec–Jan. Admission charge.

Minjasafn Reykjavíkur í Árbæ (Árbæjarsafn – Reykjavik City Museum)

This open-air folk museum harks back to the Reykjavik of 100 years ago. Almost 20 wooden buildings have been carefully renovated in period-style to create a pseudo-village. Many were saved from destruction and brought here to be installed around the site of the traditional farm of Árbær that forms the heart of the museum.

All the buildings here are of architectural merit, even the ticket office, which was built by a stonemason in 1901. Lækjargata 4 (the old address is still used as the name on the site) was the first two-storeyed house in Reykjavik when it was completed in 1852, while the Blacksmith's House (1823) is the oldest house recovered from the downtown area. The two oldest buildings are the early 1820s warehouses rescued from Vopnafjörður in eastern Iceland that sit by the recreated coastal inlet with its 1930s fishing vessel.

Árbær farm first appeared in the records in the 15th century when it was owned by the religious community on Viðey (see p53) before it was taken over by the Danish Crown. The farm changed hands many times but the family of Margrét Pétursdóttir and Eyleifur Einarsson ran it from 1881 until it was finally abandoned in 1948. Many of the farm buildings were erected or expanded during their tenure.

Throughout the summer Árbær is brought alive by a team of costumed guides who live the old country life – farmers tend the land, the ladies spin and weave, and the sailors repair their boats. Old festivals are also recreated so

The café at the Tourist Office, Reykjavik

A street in Skolavörðustigur

that you can immerse yourself in old Icelandic culture.

Bus routes 5, 6, 12, 16, 25.
v/Kistuhyl 4, 110 Reykjavik. Tel: 411 6300. www.minjasafnreykjavikur.is
Open: May 29–Aug daily 10am–5pm; Sept–May 28 Mon, Wed & Fri guided tours 1pm. Admission charge.

Listasafn Reykjavikur (Reykjavik Art Museum)

The Reykajvik Art Museum, through three sites around the city, covers the whole gamut of art in Iceland.
Payment for entrance to one Art Museum building entitles admission to the other two on the same day.

Ásmundarsafn (Ásmunder Sveinsson Museum)

Ásmunder Sveinsson was one of the most important sculptors of the 20th century and this museum – the artist's self-designed, rather futuristic home and studio from 1942–50 – features over 300 of his modernist surrealist sculptures, besides 2,400 sketches, drawings and watercolours. The verdant gardens display over 30 of his monumental pieces.
Bus routes 2, 14 and 15. Sigtún, 105 Reykjavik. Tel: 553 2155.
Open: May–Sept daily 10am–4pm; Oct–Apr daily 1–4pm.
Admission charge.

City Tour

Sightseeing buses run a hop-on, hop-off service through the downtown core of Reykjavik from *May–Sept 15, 10am–4pm*, with recorded commentaries in eight languages. Tickets are valid for 24 hours. For more details *tel: 562 1011. www.re.is*

The Ásmunder Sveinsson Museum

Hafnarhús (Harbour House)

The museum's most cutting-edge gallery is housed in an old warehouse that used to belong to the harbour authority. It is basically a series of six vast connected multipurpose spaces some of which is offered as work space to artists. Other areas host regular temporary art exhibitions, while the permanent collection includes a large donation by the artist Erró (1932–). The works include pieces from throughout his modernist career.

Bus routes 1, 2, 3, 4, 5, 6, 11, 12, 13, 14 and 15. Tryggvagata 17, 101 Reykjavik. Tel: 590 1200. Open: daily 10am–5pm. Admission charge.

Kjarvalsstaðir

Inaugurated as a specialist art exhibition hall in 1973, this gallery was named after Jóhannes Sveinsson Kjarval (1885–1972),

whose career is intertwined with the rise of Icelandic nationalism in the 20th century, when his romantic landscapes inspired his fellow countrymen. Kjarval donated a selection of his work and many personal items to the city, and these form the permanent collection here – though the works on display change regularly. But Kjarvalsstaðir's main focus is temporary exhibitions featuring the best of Icelandic and international modern art.

Bus routes 11 and 13. Flókagata, 105 Reykjavik. Open: daily 10am–5pm. Tel: 552 1290. Admission charge.

Listasafn Sigurjón Ólafssonar (Sigurjón Ólafsson Museum)

Ólafsson was a contemporary of Sveinsson (*see pp24–5 & p45*) but worked in many more media than Sveinsson. He moved between the surreal and realistic genres, spanning many of the important developments in art during the 20th century. The museum is housed in his old studio set on Reykjavik's seafront and displays works by the artist in wood, metal, stone and clay, plus a selection of works by other sculptors. *Bus route 12. Laugernastangi, 105 Reykjavik. Tel: 553 2906. www.iso.is Open: Jun–Sept Tue–Sun 2–5pm, Oct–Nov & Feb–May Sat–Sun 2–5pm. Closed: Dec–Jan. Admission charge.*

Perlan

'The Pearl' is one of Reykjavik's signature attractions and in many ways it epitomises the city's offbeat personality. Once a simple collection of round water storage tanks on a small hill to the south of the downtown core, Perlan was rescued from destruction by the vision of one man who saw more in it than huge empty tin cans. Today, the tanks have been capped by a glass roof and the space inside is multifunctional, being used for conferences and exhibitions, and even weddings. One of the city's finest gastronomic restaurants, Perlan, is located on the top floor. There is also a good café. The viewing platform around the third floor offers panoramic views over the city and the bay.

The major attraction within Perlan is the **Saga Museum**, a must for all interested in Viking history and the perfect complement to your trip to the Culture House (*see pp48–9 & p55*) and the National Museum (*see pp49–50*); this museum brings to life the tales found in those genuine *Saga* documents and priceless artefacts.

The Perlan, once a collection of water tanks, has now been converted into multifunctional spaces

Almost 20 of the pivotal moments in Iceland's history are depicted here with the help of the most lifelike full-size silica figures ever produced – Ingólfur Arnarson (the first settler) and Snorri Sturluson are scarily real – and the closest attention to the authenticity of all the objects on display. The graphic details of witch-hunts, battles and beheadings, and the imaginative English commentary that accompanies each of the dioramas are captivating, and you will come away with a greater appreciation of Iceland's history in addition to being entertained. Equally interesting is the documentary film that shows the making of the figures and displays. The figures were modelled on the family and friends of the designer – so you may notice something vaguely familiar about certain individuals as you wander the streets of the city. The gift shop sells copies of Viking clothing and artefacts.

Perlan is surrounded by verdant parkland where you can take a stroll in conducive weather. An artificial geyser spouts forth on a regular basis, offering a glimpse of Iceland's natural wonders.
Perlan Öskjuhið, 105 Reykjavik. Tel: 562 0200. Open: daily

10am–9pm, summer longer hours. Admission free.
Saga Museum: Tel: 511 1517. www.sagamuseum.is. Open: daily 10am–6pm. Admission charge.

Þjóðmenningarhúsið (The Culture House)

The exhibition at the Culture House helps put Iceland's medieval manuscripts in their context as cultural objets. From here you can go on to view over 15 original medieval manuscripts and books that constitute the backbone of the country's national identity. Most of these documents were shipped to Copenhagen during Danish rule; the first manuscripts were returned to an emotional welcome in 1971 and over 1800 came back to Iceland during the 1980s and 90s.

The initial exhibition gallery does a good job of giving the background to the creation of the books including an explanation of the oral tradition during pagan times, how the *Eddas* and *Sagas* were written down when scribes arrived on the island with the coming of Christianity, and how the *Book of Settlement* – charting the development of Iceland's society – came about. There is also a

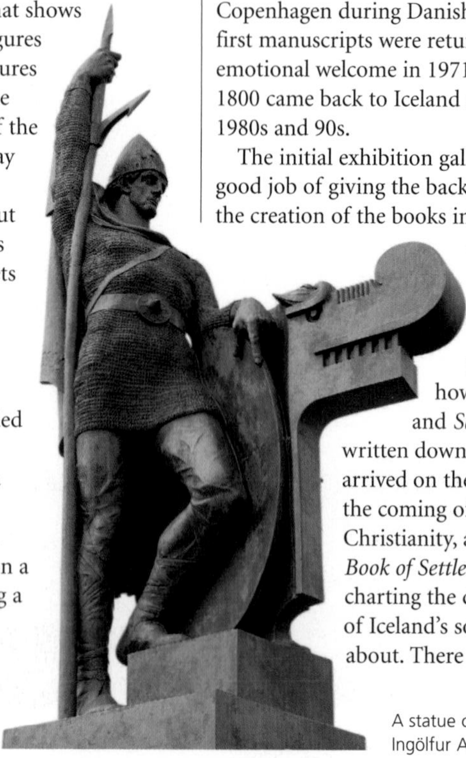

A statue of
Ingólfur Arnarson

room that has been turned into a scriptorium to explain practical details of getting words on vellum, quill-making and ink production.

The highlight of the Culture House is without doubt the original manuscripts themselves. Law codices including the *Codex Regius* of Elder Edda and an early translation of the bible are illuminating but most precious are the original *Saga* manuscripts including *Egils Saga*, the *Book of Settlement* and *Möðruvallabók* – the most important single collection of Icelandic sagas in the world.
Bus routes 1, 3, 4, 5, 6, 11, 12 and 13.
Hverfisgata 15, 101 Reykjavik.
Tel: 545 1400. Open: daily 11am–5pm.
www.thjodmenning.is
Admission charge, free Wed.

Þjóðminjasafn Íslands (National Museum of Iceland)

Re-opened in 2005 after a major expansion and restructuring, the National Museum is an impressive showcase of Iceland's rich and diverse history. Set chronologically, the collection leads from the earliest settlers to the present day in a clever combination of artefacts, oral accounts, interactive databases, film and photographic archives. Each section of the museum has a signature piece that somehow defines the larger collection around it, and an Icelandic 'resident' – a personality around whom the folkloric accounts are based.

You are first welcomed into a beautifully designed space devoted to the Viking and Celtic era leading through to the early Christian period, including two pagan burials set into the

The Cultural House houses medieval manuscripts

museum floor just as they were found by archaeologists.

Venture upstairs to continue the journey through the Danish era and into the 20th century. Depictions of the the tribulations of the 17th century include details of the witch trials of the Strandir

What's On in Reykjavik (*www.whatson.is*) is a free monthly booklet that fills you in on activities and gives you pointers for eating and entertainment. *Reykjavik City Guide*, published once every two months does much the same. There's also good background information on the latest hot-spots, concerts and trends in *Grapevine*, the free English-language newspaper produced fortnightly.

An exhibit of a Viking boat in the National Museum of Iceland

region (*p79 & pp142–3*) while the 19th century features artefacts of the crofter lifestyle including a small, single-room family home. The most dramatic single object on the second floor is a fully rigged rowing boat in the centre of the room.

The Museum employs a clever device to show the speed of Iceland's development in the last century or so. An airport luggage conveyor belt packed with everyday items from each decade loops slowly but continuously, much as the development of technology has marched onwards, forcing your attention to move from object to object. For anybody over the age of adolescence there is bound to be something that catches your attention and brings back memories. Look out for an early Björk album from the 1970s as a blast from the recent past.

Bus routes 1, 3, 4, 5, 6, 11, 12 and 14.
Suðurgata 41, 101 Reykjavik.
Tel: 530 2200. www.natmus.is
Open: May–Aug daily 10am–5pm;
Sept–Apr Tue–Sun 11am–5pm.
Admission charge.

The Volcano Show

The chances of experiencing a volcanic eruption during your stay are probably pretty fair since there is an eruption once every five years on an average. However, getting close to one is a different matter – you would not want to be anywhere near the heat, fumes and molten magma. The Volcano Show, gives you a taste of the action. Iceland's filmmakers Ósvaldur and Villi Knudsen are volcano chasers. Every time there is the smallest little rumble on the island they hotfoot it to the site with their cameras to get footage, and what they bring back is a great show, complete with plumes of fire, red-hot flows and towering steam.

Part one of the programme offers you images of every eruption on Iceland to the present day – including the *jökulhlaup* from the Grímsvötn eruption beneath Vatnajökull in 1996. This is followed by a separate one-hour part two film concentrating on the Surtsey and Heimæy eruptions in 1963 and 1973 respectively, including the human drama as the village of Heimæy has to be evacuated.

The Red Rock Cinema, Hellusund 6A, 101 Reykjavik. Tel: 845 9548 (GSM). Performances in English Jul–Aug daily 11am, 3pm and 8pm; Sept and Apr–Jun daily 3pm and 8pm; Oct–Mar 8pm. Admission charge. Tickets available at the box office 30 mins before a show or from the tourist information centre.

Lake Tjörnin

This large lake in the middle of the city is the place to come for your lunchtime picnic, that is if the birds leave you in peace to eat it. Despite its urban setting, over 30 species of wild birds make a home here, many of them migratory summer visitors. Tjörnin is flanked by some of Reykjavik's most beautiful period homes, characterised by their ornate gingerbread wooden decorative detail. The rather incongruous gun-metal grey concrete structure at the lake's southern end is the Ráðhús (Reykjavik City Hall), a controversial design at the time it was approved and still hotly disputed by locals. Visit the interior to find a 3-D visualisation of Iceland.

Ráðhús Vonarstræti. Open: Mon–Fri 8am–7pm, Sat–Sun noon–6pm. Admission free.

A view of the city from Lake Tjörnin

The Town Hall

Comfortable buses are available for excursions

EXCURSIONS FROM THE CAPITAL
Day tours

If you only have a short time in Iceland, a couple of companies run some excellent day tours from the capital to give you a taste of what you will be missing (though it really is not a substitute for a more comprehensive tour and the itinerary is pretty packed, with only limited time at each location). With all companies, you will be picked up and brought back to your hotel.

The most popular tours are the Golden Circle Route taking in Gullfoss,

Tourist Information

Tourist information about the city can be got at *The Centre, Aðalstræti 2, 101 Reykjavik. Tel: 354 590 1550. www.visitreykjavik.is* There is also the **Iceland Visitor centre** at *Lækjargata 2, 101 Reykjavik. Tel: 511 2442.*

Geysir and Þingvellir (*see pp67–8 & p73*), the Reykjanes Peninsula (*see p65 & pp74–5*), Þórsmörk, which is difficult to get to without a four-wheel drive vehicle, and a trip along the south coast to view the Sandur and Jökulsárlón glacial lake.

The following companies have a good reputation, comfortable vehicles and and English-speaking guides:
*IE – Iceland Excursions: Höfðatún 12, 105 Reykjavik. Tel: 540 1313.
www.icelandexcursions.is
Reykjavik Excursions: Vesturvör 6, 200 Kópavagur, Reykjavik. Tel: 562 1011.
www.re.is*

Viðey Island

If you want to escape the bustle of the city, head out to Viðey Island out in the bay, just a 15-minute boat ride from Reykjavik. An uninhabited island, it was once the site of a monastery and is still regarded as a religious site. Take a picnic and simply enjoy the bird life and the easy walking trails. Or visit the regular art exhibitions held through the summer.
There is a daily ferry from Reykjavik harbour at 10am returning at 1.15pm. From mid-Jun–mid-Aug there are four ferries a day from Sundahöfn harbour just north of Reykjavik centre with outward journeys at 8.30am, 1pm, 2pm, 3pm, 7pm and 9pm. Last return journey is at 9.15pm.

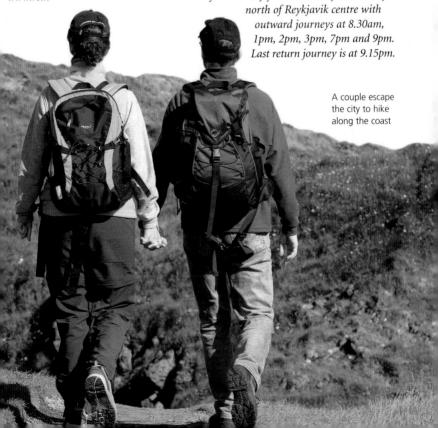

A couple escape the city to hike along the coast

Walk: Reykjavik

The best way to experience downtown Reykjavik is on foot and in a half-day-long tour you can get to see several attractions, pacing yourself with regular stops for refreshment and lunch.

Time: 4 hours with attraction visits.
Distance: 2.5km.

Start out at the Reykjavik Tourist Information Centre at Aðalstræti 2, where you can pick up background information.

1 Faxaflói

The small square in front of the Centre is the heart of the city. Look for a

sculpture of tall concrete stakes, running water and steaming plumes. This installation emulates the founding of the city when Ingólfur Arnarson cast the wooden pillars he had brought from Norway into the sea, stating that he would settle wherever they landed. They

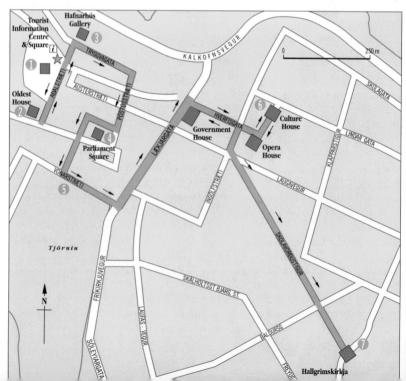

came to rest in this 'steamy' or 'smoky' bay in the Faxaflói.

Turn right out of the Tourist Centre door and walk down Aðalstræti. Just a short distance along you will come to no.10.

2 House No.10
This is considered to be the oldest wooden house in downtown Reykjavik.

Retrace your steps, cross Fischstræti and walk across the small car park directly in front of you. Across Tryggvagata you will find the Hafnarhús gallery directly in front of you.

3 Hafnarhús Gallery
This gallery is the most interesting of the three Reykjavik City Art Galleries because it is a working space in addition to being a space for hosting avant-garde exhibitions.

Turn left out of the Gallery and walk down Tryggvagata past the Kolaportið warehouse building. Ahead to the right you will see the Bæjarins Betzu Pýlsur kiosk. If you are peckish, stop here for a snack. Turn right at this junction and walk down Póstússtræti. Continue across Austerstræti to reach a small square, which is often the site for temporary exhibitions.

4 The Square
The square is graced with a statue of Jón Sigurðsson (1811–1879), the father of Icelandic nationalism, while at the far flank is the Alþing (Parliament), a curious amalgam of 18th-century stone and 20th-century glass buildings.

Walk down the narrow alleyway to the right of the Parliament and cross

Vonarstræti to reach Tjörnin.

5 Tjörnin
Reykjavik's beautiful lake is always full of birds so carry some breadcrumbs to feed them. You can then make up your own mind as to whether the sleek lines of the Ráðhús (Reykjavik City Hall) enhance or detract from the chocolate-box wooden period homes that are its close neighbours.

From the eastern corner of Tjörnin (the other end of Vonarstræti from Ráðhús), turn left and walk down Lækjargata. You will re-cross Austerstræti and on your right you will see a long white wooden building, the offices of Iceland's Prime Minister. Cross Lækjargata at the traffic light here, turn right and then left on Hverfisgata where you will find Þjóðmenningarhúsið (Culture House) about 50m up on the left.

6 Þjóðmenningarhúsið (Culture House)
Enjoy the magnificent medieval manuscripts and learn more about Iceland's *Eddas* and *Sagas*.

From Þjóðmenningarhúsið cross over Hverfisgata, walk right, then left down Ingólfstræti past the Opera House, to Laugavegur, Reykjavik's main shopping street. Turn left here, then right on Skolavörðustigur, the Arts District of the city, and walk uphill to Hallgrimskirkja.

7 Hallgrimskirkja
Have your photograph taken in front of Leifur Eiríksson's statue before heading up the church steeple for panoramic views over the city (in good weather).

Around the Capital

The region around Reykjavik sees more visitors than any other area of Iceland apart from the capital itself. There are two reasons for this. Firstly, it is an easy drive from the capital for those on a short stay or for those who don't want to move out of a city hotel. Secondly the region has many attractions that give a flavour of the country without having to make a full tour of the island.

A road leading out of Reykjavik

The two areas closest to Reykjavik are the rolling farmland immediately east of the city where the so-called 'big three' attractions can be found – so called because they are amongst the most visited and are in close proximity to one another – and the Reykjanes Peninsula, a long finger of volcanic land pointing westward, just below the capital.

Akranes

The only real reason for visiting Akranes is the **Akranes Museum Centre**, opened in 1959 and housed on the site of an old manor farm, Garðar, that features in the *Sagas* as the home of Irish settlers in the

Tourists click photos of Akranes

9th century and Guðný Böðvarsdóttir circa 1200. It was a centre of Christianity from the first days of conversion and the parsonage operated until the late 19th century.

Today the site has a collection of buildings that tell the story of the development of the town from these humble beginnings through to the early 1900s. The oldest wooden house in the town, erected in 1875, was moved here in 2002 to sit alongside an old fish-drying shed, a boathouse and ketch built in Hull (UK) in 1885. Fróðá's house was used by sail and net-makers in the 1930s. There is an old school house, Geirsstaðir, christened Geirsstaðir University by the locals. The folk collection is housed in a separate building and is a fascinating and eclectic mixture of artefacts, large and small, charting the development of the town and showing how daily life changed over the centuries, including an unusual display of medical tools and equipment. Incorporated into the whole are some interesting but seemingly unrelated collections: the Land Survey exhibition which will attract lovers of geography and show developments in the science

since records began; there is the comprehensive show of rocks in Mineral Kingdom; the Sport in Iceland collection which may be the least interesting for outsiders as luminaries on the international stage are relatively few.
The Akranes Museum Centre: off Graðagrund. Tel: 431 5566. www.museum.is. Open: daily May 15–Sept 15, 10am–6pm; Sept 16–May 14, 1–6pm. Admission charge.

Bessastaðir

The site of an ancient manor farm less than 10km from central Reykjavik, the complex at Bessastaðir set amidst coastal lowland and lava fields is now the official residence of the President of Iceland.

First mentioned in the *Íslendinga Saga*, the farm was owned by storyteller Snorri Sturluson (*see pp28–9*); it passed to the Norwegian throne and remained a royal estate until it was bought for a school in 1805. The present building is one of the oldest in Iceland having been erected in 1761. It became the President's official residence in 1941. There is also a small church (1777) and a graveyard on the site.
Church: open to the public daily 9am–5pm except when the President is in residence. Admission free. House and grounds private property.

Around Reykjavik

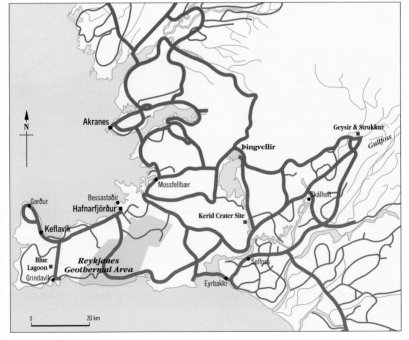

Bláa Lónið (Blue Lagoon)

Probably Iceland's most famous tourist attraction, the Blue Lagoon is a beautiful complex of geothermal pools fed by the continental rift. Perhaps it ruins the romance, but the waters travel through the Svartsengi power plant before they hit the pools – ever practical, the Icelanders! The lagoon is revered for its pools, which are set against a black volcanic basalt backdrop – the whole concept is Caribbean-meets-geothermal springs and it is unique. The waters are also rich in mud that has been proved to be highly beneficial for one's skin. You can spend hours here just lounging in the shallows, taking a massage or sunbathing – yes it is possible in Iceland. The restaurant has an excellent reputation, so take a break for a long lunch. The waters are not good to

precious metals, so leave your jewellery back in your hotel safe for the day.

In the same complex as Blue Lagoon is a fascinating attraction that takes you to the heart of Iceland's continental rift. This is a must for anyone interested in plate tectonics and the science of how the world was created. The 18 information screens at **Gjáin** (The Rift), set amongst the very rock under discussion, tell you everything you need to know about geothermal energy, plus volcanoes and glaciers.

Bláa Lónið. Blue Lagoon Road, Grindavík. Tel: 354 420 8800. www.bluelagoon.is. Open: mid May–Aug daily 9am–9pm; Sept–mid May 10am–8pm. Admission charge.
Gjáin: details as Blue Lagoon. Open: May 15–Aug daily 10am–7pm; Sept–May 14, 10am–4pm. Admission charge.

Enjoy a natural spa treatment at the Blue Lagoon

The Garðskagi Lighthouse

Eyrbakki

Once home to the largest community in southwestern Iceland, this small coastal town has a large selection of late 19th- and early 20th-century architecture, plus a couple of important historical landmarks. Husið and Assistenta Husið are two connected structures that were ordered from a kit catalogue from Scandinavia. Husið was erected in 1765 and is one of the oldest wooden structures on the island, while Assistenta Husið was added over a century later, in 1881. Husið now houses the Árnes Folk Museum with exhibitions about the history of the town.

Eyrbakki was the home of one of Iceland's greatest Viking explorers, Bjarni Herjólfsson, who sailed west in the 980s and was probably the first

European to spot the North American coast. His tales caught the imagination of Leifur Eirikson, who named this new discovery Vinland.

Husið. Hafnarbrú 3. Tel: 354 483 1504. www.husid.is. Open: Jun–Aug daily 11am–5pm; Apr–May & Sept–Oct 2–5pm; by arrangement rest of the year. Admission charge.

Garður

Set on the northernmost point of the Reykjanes Peninsula, Garður is a small village surrounded by some of the best birdwatching landscape on the island. The Garðskagi Lighthouse erected in 1944 on the site of an earlier phare (lighthouse) marks the most northerly point, and is the tallest lighthouse in Iceland.

Tourists gather to watch Strukker

The Byggðasafnið á Garðskaga (Garður Peninsula Historical Museum) has some highly unusual artefacts; objects related to shoe-making which was an important industry for many years, and fishing that thrived here as in many places across the island, an egg-hatching machine, and milking equipment. Pride of place goes to the engines dating from 1924 to 1977, collected with love and devotion by Guðni Ingimundarson. Garður also has an interesting church, Útskálakirkja, finished in 1863.

Byggðasafnið á Garðskaga.

Tel: 422 7108. Open: May–Aug daily 1–5pm; by appointment at other times. Admission charge.

Geysir and Strukkur

The spectacular gush of hot steamy water rising regularly through a small hole in the ground was called Geysir by Icelanders. Eventually the name became synonymous with a hot water spout, and Geysir became geyser in the English language. Today the original Geysir can still be visited, though the 'old man' is well past his prime. Throughout the 20th century many attempts were made to make the spout gush on command and eventually it stopped completely – it is now little more than a constant steamy emission. A new pretender has now taken over the throne, only metres from the last king. Strukker is every bit its father's son, spouting every 5–7 minutes as high as 15m into the air – though the height varies with the strength of the pressure below the surface. Crowds of all ages gather enthralled, waiting for the next expulsion, which is always accompanied by a hiss of steam.

Around the two geyser sites is an area of geothermic activity with fumaroles and hot steamy springs. It is a good introduction to what makes Iceland special in relation to volcanic activity.

Grindavík

A modern fishing town with state-of-the-art plants, Grindavík is worth a visit for Saltfisksetur Íslands (the Saltfish Museum). This new museum complex explains the development of salting as a means of preserving the fish and covers the heyday of salting in the area around the start of the last century. Real saltfish are placed around the exhibition to bring home the smell and sight of the product, and these are complemented by dioramas and photographs that document the processes. You can also enjoy fishy snacks at the café on site.

The town's main church, Grindavíkurkirkja, is one the strangest on the island. Inaugurated in 1982, it has the aesthetic qualities of a local factory combined with a municipal swimming pool. Only the small cross atop the white painted water-tower-like steeple indicates that it is a place of worship.

The Blue Lagoon (*see p58*) lies within Grindavík municipal boundaries.

Saltfisksetur Íslands. Hafnargata 12a. Tel: 420 1190. www.saltfisksetur.is Open: daily 11am–6pm. Admission charge.

Gullfoss

Iceland's most visited 'foss' is also its most spectacular. It is an 'L' shaped waterfall with a curtain cascade of white water and a sheer drop into a narrow fissure that directs a drenching spray and deafening noise in the direction of bystanders.

Gullfoss means 'golden falls' in Icelandic. No-one is really sure why it has been given this name. Some say that the sunlight playing on the water give the spray a golden sheen, which is true enough – but only on a bright day! In winter curtains of ice form around the

The Saltfish Museum in Grindavík

The spectacular Gullfoss waterfall

still active falls, changing the scene into a white wonderland.
Open access. Admission free.

Hafnarfjörður

One of Iceland's most important fishing towns, Hafnarfjörður products find their way to tables across the world. It has also been a trading town since the 1300s, thanks to the fine natural harbour that gives Hafnarfjörður its name. Today the suburbs of Reykjavik have muscled their way against the boundary, but Hafnarfjörður has a strong civic pride that sets it apart from 'the city' just up the road.

There are a quite a few surprises here, not least the jumble of brightly coloured façades of homes that rise above the harbour. Every year in mid-June the town is invaded by hundreds of 'Vikings' dressed in full regalia for the annual 'Viking Festival' that celebrates all things Norse. It is said that some of these people live their life full-time, wearing traditional clothes and celebrating pagan festivals. The **Viking Village** is the centre of festival activities – this wooden pavilion carved with dragons' heads and other symbolic images is the place to taste a bit of Viking life, whatever time of year you may visit. It hosts Viking banquets with wenches and warriors, saga recitals and hearty singing. You can stay in the comfortable hotel if the mead and ale get the better of you.

Byddðasafn Hafnarfjörður (Hafnarfjörður Museum)

This collection of three old wooden houses now form the town museum. The permanent 'Thus it was…' exhibition tells the story of the history of the town from its first settlers to the development of the fishing industry. There is a special gallery dedicated to the British sojourn in Iceland. **Sívertsen House,** the oldest of the three and home to one of the town's most influential families, is furnished in 19th-century period style. In contrast, **Siggubær's Pakkhúsið**, built in 1902, has displays relating to the life of a working family a hundred years later.

The town has an excellent gallery, **Hafnaborg,** that hosts ever-changing exhibitions featuring Icelandic artists. This is yet another venue that has on display the rich modern art of the island.

Hafnarfjörður is said to be a stronghold of elves and little people who hide in the caves and lava holes around the town, so keep your eyes open as you tour around!

Bus routes from Reykjavik 1, 21 and 22.
The Viking Village: Strandgata 55.
Tel: 565 1213. www.fjorukrain.is
Byddðasafn Hafnarfjörður: Vesturgata 8.
Tel: 585 5780. www.hafnarfjordur.is
Pakkhúsið: open: Jun–Aug daily
11am–5pm; Sept–May Sat–Sun
11am–7pm.
Sívertsen House: open: Jun–Aug daily
11am–5pm; Sept–May by request.
Siggubær's Pakkhúsið: open: Jun–Aug
Sat–Sun 11am–5pm, winter by request.
Admission charge.
Hafnaborg: Strandgata 34.
Tel: 354 555 0080. www.hafnarborg.is
Open: Wed–Mon 11am–5pm.
Admission charge.

Keflavík

People mostly know Keflavík because it is the site of the international airport but the town has several attractions beyond the regular landings and takeoffs of airplanes. The largest town on the peninsula, it is prosperous not only because of the airport but also due to its proximity to the large American-dominated NATO base.

The town's port is home to the *Íslendingur*, an authentic recreation of the original Viking ship that sailed from Iceland to the east coast of the United States in the year 2000 in the wake of and in celebration of the Viking explorers. You can also go out on whale-watching trips from the harbour.

The cultural centre at **Duus Hús** has one of the most unusual collections in Iceland. The miniature boats on display are examples drawn from the entire history of Iceland's fishing fleet and were brought together by a former trawler captain for whom these models were a passion.

There is a small folk museum in **Ytri-Njarðvík**, a reconstructed turf farmhouse in neighbouring Njarðvík, but it is not open regular hours so consult the tourist office if you would like to make a visit.

Duus Hús: Duusgata 2-10.
Tel: 421 3796. Open: daily 11am–6pm.
Admission charge.
Ytri-Njarðvík: Stekkjarkot. Tel: 421 3796.
Open: by appointment. Admission charge.

Whale-watching boats

Visitors try to capture geothermal activity

Kerid Crater Site

A small but perfectly formed crater sits beside the main road between Selfoss and Laugervatn, making it one of the easiest to visit for those who don't wish to walk far. There is a viewing platform but it is best not to walk around the rim as the ground is loose and the sides rather steep.

Open access. Admission free.

Mossfellbær

This small town just north of the capital, almost part of Reykjavik's greater agglomeration, has little to attract visitors except for the fact that it was home to one of Iceland's greatest 20th-century sons.

Pride of place in Mossfellbær goes to **Gljúfrasteinn**, home of Nobel Prize winner and author Halldór Laxness, and now open to the public as the **Laxness Museum**. The house was built in 1945 in the plain functional style of that time. Halldór spent his last years here and the rooms have been preserved as the author had them, including the study upstairs with his books and personal items. This room also has a collection of works of art by his peers, amongst them Jóhannes Kjarval (*see p46*). The museum includes a multimedia presentation about the life of the author set against the larger socio-economic context that defined his work.

Gljúfrasteinn: 270 Mossfellbær. Tel: 586 8066. www.gljufrasteinn.is. Open: Jun–Aug daily 9am–5pm; Sept–May Tue–Sun 10am–5pm. Admission charge.

Reykjanes Geothermal Area

One of Iceland's most active geothermal areas, the Reykjanes peninsula sits on the westernmost landward section of the continental rift. It is volcanically active – as witnessed by the numerous and wide-spread lava fields and geothermic fields that feed the Blue Lagoon (*see p58 & p75*) in addition to heating local homes.

Besides the steaming pools that feed the Lagoon, there are two other areas of natural geothermal activity; Gunnuhver west of Grindavík, and close to the southwest point of the peninsula; and Seltún, east of the same town. These are generally much less visited than the Geysir and Strukkur site so you can spend time here simply marvelling at nature's wonder.

Just north of the Seltún field is Krysuvikurkirkja, a diminutive black painted church dating from 1861; sadly, though, it is rarely open.

Open access both areas. Admission free.

Reykjanes Geothermal Area

Note
Just so you don't get confused, the two towns of Keflavik and Narðvik now market themselves as Reykjanesbær. This name appears on many brochures and advertising hoardings in the area but it is a new epithet.

Skálholt Cathedral is an important attraction in the region

Selfoss

The largest town in southern Iceland, Selfoss is the centre of Iceland's dairy industry but has little to hold a tourist. Just a little way southwest of the city, on the Ölfusá River that the town flanks, is the Flói Nature Reserve, an important marshland environment for migratory bird populations.

Skálholt Cathedral

The southern seat of the Catholic bishops of Iceland – whose northern seat is at Hólar (*see p95*) – this site was of paramount importance to the religious life of the country in the years 1056–1550. The last Catholic bishop, Jón Arason, along with two of his sons,

The Bridge Between Two Continents

This narrow metal bridge spans the narrow divide between the North American and European plates and you can walk between the two without carrying a passport! Once you've crossed, head to the information office at Reykjanesbær (Hafnargargötu 57, Kefkavik) to get a certificate of the event! *The bridge is situated south of Keflavik off route 425. Open access. Admission free.*

was beheaded here in 1550 on the orders of the Danish Crown, in a final act to put down the Catholic faith and herald the victory of the Lutheran Reformation.

The original cathedral on the site was taken down in the 18th century and today's church, though of course a Protestant place of worship, did not replace it until the 1950s. The site has a small museum related to the Reformation, a plaque to Jón, and the tomb of another bishop, Páll Jónsson, who was a religious leader in the early 13th century, which was found during the extensive and still ongoing archaeological excavations.

The Icelandic Lutheran Church runs the surrounding complex as camp and educational facility for children.

Þingvellir (see also p53)

(see also p53)

Visitors from other countries might wonder about the effect this area has on Icelanders, but there is still a reason why it is among the most visited sites on the island. The park is breathtakingly beautiful with its rocks, rivers and

The entrance to 'friends' wood' (Vinaskógar)

meadowland – it is one of the few landscapes in the country that is on a human scale rather than being humbling in its vastness.

Þingvellir was the original site of the historic Icelandic Parliament, the Alþing, the first democratic governmental structure that the world had seen when it was founded in 930. The pastureland that was the meeting place of the Parliament sits in a wide valley by the banks of Þingvallavatn Lake and directly on the continental rift, where North America and Europe are gradually moving apart at the rate of a millimetre a year.

You can stand on the **Lögberg** or 'Law Rock' where proclamations of the laws passed were made; the site is marked by a flagpole. There are also a few remains of numerous *búðir*, where the delegates would stay during the proceedings.

Modern Icelanders consider this site the symbolic heart of the country and gather here in thousands on important occasions such as the founding day of independent Iceland in 1944, and in 2000 to celebrate a millennium of Christianity.

Declared a UNESCO World Heritage Site in 2004, it includes an old parsonage and a national graveyard where several luminaries now rest. The most traditional building is **Þingvellabær**, a farmhouse built in 1930 to commemorate the first meeting of the Alþing. The farmhouse recalls the fact that in 930 these fields were part of private farmland owned by a settler. Þingvellabær is now used as a summer residence by the Prime Minister of Iceland.

The **National Park information office** has information about the history and the landscape of the region. There are many easy and enjoyable walks that are accessible to even the most physically unfit.

To the northwest of the site of the Alþing is the western wall of the continental rift along the Almannagjá (Everyman's) fault. The **Hakið Interpretive Centre** screens a regular video show explaining how the fault works. The most exciting part of this visit is to walk on the wall of the fissure itself – standing on North American land and looking eastward to Europe only a few hundred metres away across the continental divide.

South of the Alþing site is Þingvallatn, over 80sq km of fresh water sitting on the rift. There are a couple of volcanic islands and a geothermal field on route 360, on the western flank. Close by is a small copse of trees surrounded by a wall and marked by a phalanx of national flags. This is **Vinaskógar** or 'friends' wood'. All the trees planted here are gifts to the incumbent President of Iceland

from foreign dignitaries. The grove was started on the 60th birthday of President Vigdís Finnbogardóttir with a gift of several birch trees from an Irish Ambassadorial delegation.

Þingvellir Visitor Centre: www.thingvellir.is. Open: May–Sept daily 8.30am–8pm. Admission free.

Hakið Interpretive Centre: open: Jun–Aug daily 9am–7pm; Apr–May & Sept–Oct 9am–5pm; Nov–Mar Sat–Sun 9am–5pm. Admission free.

Vinaskógar: open access. Admission free.

Þingvellabær is popular for its breathtaking landscape

Pagan Religion

Religion was an important aspect of the daily life of Vikings. A panoply of gods controlled their everyday lives, the seasons and the results of their raids and conquests. The pagan religion of the Vikings, though long dead, has left behind a legacy. Many of the days of the week in the English calendar are named after these northern gods who used to be worshipped by the Norse and their Saxon cousins.

How the world was created

According to the religion of the Vikings, the universe was made up of many regions. To the south was a bright warm land where the fire giant Muspel had his domain. In the north was a place of cold and darkness ruled by a goddess called Hel. This was the place where those who did not die the death of a warrior would spend eternity.

At the dawn of time there was nothing between these two realms but empty space. However, along came Ymir who brought forth the Norse gods and giants. The chief god Odin killed Ymir and created Midgard or 'Middle Earth' – the realm that filled the void – from Ymir's remains.

After Odin created Middle Earth, he built Asgard, the home of the gods. There was a home for each of them plus a special place for the Viking warriors who died in battle. The place was called Valhalla. A special force of women warriors called Valkyries made decisions about who would be victorious in battle and who could be admitted into Valhalla.

Eventually, time would end when the giants of the cold land and the giants of the hot lands would clash in cataclysmic battle. This was called Ragnarok, the end of the worlds – except that the cycle would then start all over again.

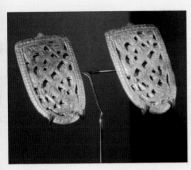

THE GODS

Odin

Chief of the gods, Odin had gained wisdom and cunning by drinking from the sacred spring. The runes (*see p17*) were revealed to Odin and they became magical symbols and a secret code. Odin's Saxon name was Woden, from which the English Wednesday is derived.

Thor

Son of Odin, Thor was the strongest of the gods and is depicted holding a hammer. Thunder was his weapon and he was often entreated by humans during vicious storms. Thor is put through many trials by the evil 'world serpent' who tried to usurp his power. They met in a final tumultuous battle at Ragnarok. Thor was remembered in the English Thursday.

Freya

Freya was the goddess of love and extremely beautiful. She is remembered in the English Friday.

Tyr

Another son of Odin, Tyr was the god of war. His Saxon name was Tiu and he gave his name to the English Tuesday.

Sol and Mani

Sol and Mani were the sun and the moon, set in the sky by Odin when he created Middle Earth. Both drove chariots in great haste across the sky because they were being chased by evil wolves. When Ragnarok arrived the wolves would catch them both, and day and night would cease to exist. In Saxon the sun and moon were called Sunne and Mona, giving us the English Sunday and Monday.

Facing page: Gudridur statue;
This page above left: A pagan brooch;
right: Troll dolls

SO THAT'S WHY!

The Viking pagan midwinter celebration was known as Jul, and is carried on in our modern yuletide greetings around Christmas time.

Drive: The Golden Circle Route

Iceland's Golden Circle links the three main attractions close to Reykjavik in one enjoyable day trip. While the circuit is a popular tour group choice, we have added a few extra attractions in this self-drive itinerary that you won't be able to enjoy by bus.

Time: 8 hours.

Distance: 250km.

Start out from Reykjavik after a hearty breakfast. Leave by the Miklbraut, then Reykjanesbraut, following the signs to route 1 and Selfoss. Once on route 1, head southeast, initially following the same signs. After 17km you will pass signs for the Svínaharun Ski area to your left. After a further 16km you will reach Hveragerði.

1 Hveragerði

Hveragerði is a small town that makes a living from geothermally heated glass houses. You can visit Eden (*Austermörk 2; tel: 483 4900; open: summer daily 9am–11pm, winter 9am–7pm; admission free*), Iceland's answer to a tropical greenhouse.

Continue on route 1 for another 11km and just before reaching Selfoss turn left on route 35. Drive on and after 8km you will cross the River Sog. Soon you will find the car park of the Kerid Crater site on your right.

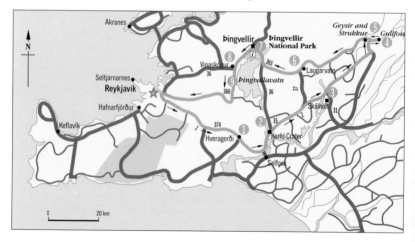

2 Kerid Crater

This small crater site is a suitable stop for volcano enthusiasts.

Continue north on route 35 for another 23km and then turn right on to route 31. Just a couple of kilometres after the junction, Skálholt comes into view across the fields on the right.

3 Skálholt

This Lutheran complex was built in the last few years but stands on the site of a Catholic Bishopric. Visit the 20th-century church to find items from those earlier times, including the tomb of an 11th-century bishop.

Return to route 35 and turn right. The road becomes increasingly more rural and asphalt turns to dirt on short sections. Keep following the signs for Gullfoss (you will pass the Geysir site on the left but we will return here soon).

4 Gullfoss

Gullfoss is an impressive sight but the sound of the waters hits you well before the falls come into view. The water fans out over two small curtain falls before dropping into a narrow chasm and disappearing from view.

Leave Gullfoss by the same road as you came and this time stop at Geysir.

5 Geysir

Geysir is the most famous geyser in the world but now it is a spent force. Strukkur, however, performs at least once every 10 minutes, day or night. Enjoy the surrounding geothermal pools and flumes.

Turn left out of the Geysir car park and follow the signs to Laugarvatn on route 37. Laugarvatn is 37km from Gullfoss.

6 Laugarvatn

Laugarvatn is a small summer resort with a spa that is popular with people from the capital.

At Laugarvatn turn right on route 365 in the direction of Þingvellir National Park. This mostly dirt road leads you through some wild landscapes. After 16km you will reach the junction of route 36. Take a right turn here. You will see the Information Centre and car park signposted on the left after 8km.

7 Þingvellir

The buildings at Þingvellir, the 'Parliament fields' are picture-perfect. Enjoy taking a stroll on the Continental Rift and the views across the lake.

Return from the car park to route 36. Turn left and follow the road. After 9km you will see Vinaskógur on the right.

8 Vinaskógur

Vinaskógur or 'friends' wood', is a copse of trees given as gifts to the President of Iceland by visiting dignitaries.

Just beyond Vinaskógur turn left on route 360.

9 Þingvallavatn

Route 360 skirts the shores of Lake Þingvallavatn in a rollercoaster ride past numerous small summer cabins owned by wealthy Icelanders from Reykjavik, and a small geothermal site. There are good lake views between the shrubs and copses.

After 10km there is a right turn to Reykjavik over the Mosfellsheiði.

Drive: The Reykjanes Peninsula

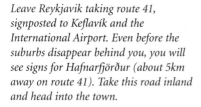

Leaving the capital behind and heading southwest brings you face to face with the real Iceland – a country of volcanoes and fishing, and a land of small-town living.

Time: 8 hours.

Distance: 190km.

Leave Reykjavik taking route 41, signposted to Keflavík and the International Airport. Even before the suburbs disappear behind you, you will see signs for Hafnarfjörður (about 5km away on route 41). Take this road inland and head into the town.

1 Hafnarfjörður

Hafnarfjörður has a large and busy harbour and you will usually see some activity in the mornings with boats landing their catches. Visit the Hafnarfjörður Museum.

Return to route 41 and follow the signs for Keflavík. You will pass a municipal hoarding announcing that you are arriving in Reykjanesbær; after 25km you can turn right into the town.

2 Keflavík and Njarðvík

Keflavík and neighbouring Njarðvík

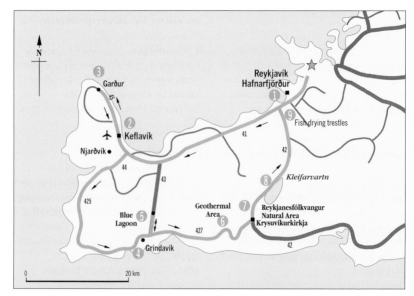

seem to meet each other across the wide bay that used to separate them. Head to the harbour to see if you can spot *Íslendingur*, the recreation of an original Viking ship.

Return to route 41 and head west (left turn). You will pass the turning to the airport on the left; then take route 45 in the direction of Garður.

3 Garður Peninsula Historical Museum

Garður Peninsula Historical Museum makes an interesting diversion, or you can head to the coast for some bird-spotting.

Retrace your drive past the airport and the Keflavík turning and, after 11km, take a right turn at the junction for route 44; 4km ahead, turn left on route 425 in the direction of Grindavík. This route leads you through rugged coastal landscape before you reach the town.

4 Saltfish Museum

Visit the Saltfish Museum in Grindavík.

From Grindavík it is only 6km or so along route 43 to the Blue Lagoon.

5 Blue Lagoon

Stopping for a relaxing swim at the Blue Lagoon might sabotage your plans for the rest of the trip. You could spend an hour or two, or come back later for a fuller session.

Return south to Grindavík and take route 427 east. Few tourists head this way even though it is so close to the capital. After 20km you will see a geothermal area on your left.

6 Geothermal Area

This is one of the more interesting geothermal regions visually because the plumes, pools and boiling pots rise up the hillside.

Continue on route 427 for another 3km and you will reach the junction of route 42. Turn left here. Just beyond the junction you will see a small church on the left.

7 Krysuvikurkirkja

This is Krysuvikurkirkja, one of the oldest wooden churches in Iceland and now a national monument.

Route 42 runs through the heart of the Reykjanesfólkvangur Natural Area. It is a seemingly desolate place but has some good walking routes. After another 5km Kleifarvartn comes into view on the right.

8 Kleifarvartn

This starkly beautiful lake is set amidst jet-black rocks.

Continue on route 42 which eventually leads you back to the southern suburbs of Hafnarfjörður. Just before you reach the urban sprawl you will pass rows of wooden latticework on either side of the road.

9 Fish-drying trestles

Drying fish in the open air is becoming less popular now but before the introduction of salting and freezing, it was the main method of preserving the product.

Route 42 will eventually meet route 41 where you can make a right turn following signposts for the capital, Reykjavik.

Snæfellsnes and the Westfjords

Iceland's northwestern corner is a region shrouded in myths and of contrasting landscapes with solitary farmhouses, hidden valleys and indomitable cliffs. Snæfellsnes is easily reached from Reykjavik, whereas the Westfjords involves a serious journey – but the rewards for those who venture there are many!

A fisherman's cottage

The Snæfellsnes Peninsula points westward like a finger. It is a narrow yet varied world of cliffs, valleys and tiny towns set in the shadow of the brooding and mysterious Snæfellsjökull, a newly dormant volcano.

The southern coastline of Snæfellsnes has some of Iceland's most dramatic lava fields stretching from the extinct crater to the sea. The rich blanket of mosses and lichens growing on the lunar landscape changes colour throughout the day, and the weird rock formations have given rise to tales of trolls and little people who are said to inhabit the numerous caves.

The northern coast of the peninsula is a total contrast, with rounded hills and sweeping lowland meadows forming the southern shore of the vast Breiðafjörður inlet and Hvammsfjörður, a region of scattered islands and islets. The mountain of **Kirkjufell** (463m) with its glorious curves is considered the most beautiful and is typical of the vista.

To the north of the Snæfellsnes, the Westfjords is the oldest part of Iceland. The landmass owes its glorious vistas to glaciation. Sheer cliffs that rise over 100m directly from the ocean are tabletopped by thousands of hectares of upland moors carpeted with alpine tundra and often shrouded in mist. The Westfjords is sparsely populated with a handful of towns clinging limpet-like to the valley floors. The many abandoned farms stand witness to the recent depopulation and make the Westfjords seem all the more wild.

Linking the two regions is the low-lying meadowland of the Dalir, an area

---

0   100 km

Bolungarvík

Ísafjörður

Fjallfoss

N

Holmavík

Flatay

Kirkjufell
(463m)   Hvammsfjörður

Ólafsvík   Stykkishólmur
Öndverðarnes
Point   Helgafell
Snæfellsjökull   **Búðir**
1446m   Arnastapi

rich in *Saga* history, where the Sturlungs – who controlled half of Iceland during the 13th century – had their power base.

Arnastapi

This tiny collection of buildings set around a small rocky cove is one of the best places along the coast to stop for birdwatching. In the summer, the cliffs and offshore basalt stacks look like high-rise apartment blocks for seagoing birds as they circle above your head in their thousands. On the clifftop stands a sturdy stone sculpture by Ragnar Kjartansson representing Bárður Snæfellsás, the guardian spirit of the region.

The 526m-high **Stapafell** behind the cove is reputedly home to mischievous trolls. A road to the east of the hill leads up to the snowline at **Snæfellsjökull**.

You can walk along the cliffs west of town for around 2.5km to reach **Hellnar**, a small fishing town, passing some of the region's most dramatic volcanic landscapes where the power of the ocean has eroded the lava flows into surreal columns and razor-edged ridges. Hellnar was the home of Guðriður Þorbjarnardóttir who, according to accounts, was the first European woman to give birth on North American soil when she travelled to Vinland in 1004. A small plaque close to the main road marks the location of the family farm.

Búðir

A tiny anchorage on the southern coast of the Snæfellsnes, Búðir sits in the heart of a protected area of a volcanic lava field. There is nothing left of the village now save a tiny 19th-century church,

one of the few on Iceland that was built by a private individual without the authority of the Icelandic Lutheran Church. Walk past the church to the black sand beach, which stretches east around the peninsula and is one of the finest of its kind on the island.

Bolungarvík

One of Iceland's oldest fishing communities, Bolungarvík hugs the water's edge in the shadow of Traðarhyna Hill to the northwest of Ísafjörður.

The town's **Náttúrugripasafn Bolungarvíkur** (Natural History Museum) offers a collection of stuffed birds and animals including an unfortunate polar bear shot as it made a diversion from the snowfields of Greenland.

The more interesting **Ósvör** brings the salt-fishing industry to life. Housed in an old fisherman's hut, the museum includes everyday artefacts and a salt-fishing shed that smells like the real thing!

There is a monument to Einar Guðfinsson (1898–1985) on the waterfront. The businessman was responsible for the economic viability of the town.

Náttúrugripasafn Bolungarvíkur: Vitastig 3 and Aðalstræti 21. Tel: 456 7005. www.nave.is (Icelandic only). Open: Mon–Fri 9am–5pm, Sat–Sun 1–5pm. Admission charge. Ósvör: Safn-gömul verbúð. Tel: 892 1615. Open: daily noon–6pm. Admission charge.

The 100m-high Fjallfoss waterfall

Fjallfoss

The Westfjords largest waterfall is easy to find. The main road runs right by and there is ample parking at the base. The 100m-high and very broad falls that break into several separate white cascades are also known as Dynjandi, meaning 'resounding', for their sound that can be heard throughout the surrounding valleys.

Flatay

The only populated island in Breiðafjörður, Flatay was home to some of Iceland's first settlers when a community of Irish monks established a monastery here in 1172. They did not stay long, moving to Helgafell as early as 1184. The town became an official trading post in 1777 and was a cultural centre during the 19th century housing Iceland's first library, but it is a sleepy backwater today. There are many period houses to enjoy in the town and the parish church features a fresco by contemporary artist Baltasar. You can also head out on foot to enjoy easy walks.

You can reach Flatay from Stykkishólmur (*see p84*) on the northern Snaefellsnes Peninsula or Brjánslækur on the southern coast of the Wesfjords on the daily ferry *Baldur* (*www.saeferdir.is; departures 9am and 4pm*).

To the west of Flatay are the waters of Breiðafjörður scattered with small islands that are home to large populations of sea birds.

Holmavík

This one-horse town on the southeastern coast of the Westfjords could be easily bypassed were it not for a fascinating little exhibition. The **Galdrasýning á Ströndum** (Icelandic Sourcery and Witchcraft Exhibition) is the result of one man's obsession with the tradition of witchcraft on Iceland. The museum explains the traditions of sorcery – which, unusually, was controlled by men here in contrast to witchcraft in other countries which tended to be the women's domain – and charts the witchcraft accusations and trials that swept Iceland, and particularly the Strandir region (*see pp142–3*), during the 17th century. In a

frenzy that matched the zeal of the Inquisition, over 20 people were burnt at the stake and many more flogged. More often than not, the accusations related to Norse pagan practices and rituals carried on through the ages, but some seemed to have a 'supernatural' basis.

The museum has some unusual artefacts including an ancient 'blood stone' where sacrifices (of animals) were made; there are also modern recreations of certain so-called magical practices that took place in these parts. The exhibition is best experienced with the English commentary (*extra charge*) which does an excellent job of explaining the background to the events, and the role that magic and superstition played in the lives of Icelanders at that time.

The museum has a second exhibit, the Sorcerer's Cottage, at Bjarnarfjörður, 30km north into the Strandir, and there are plans to open others around the region.

Galdrasýning á Ströndum: Höfðagata 8–10. Tel: 451 3525. Open: Jun–Aug daily 10am–6pm, rest of the year by request. Admission charge.

Displays at the Witchcraft Museum

The historic houses of Ísafjörður

Hvammsfjörður

Hvammsfjörður forms a narrow inlet at the southeastern head of Breiðafjörd. This was one of the centres of action during the old *Saga* (*see pp28–9*) days. Snorri Sturluson (*see pp28–9*) was born in the countryside at the head of the fjord, and the rolling farmland was the setting for the *Laxædala Saga* telling tales of several generations of Icelandic farmers.

Hvammsfjörður has hundreds of islets, some mere sentinel rocks, that play host to some of the richest bird populations on Iceland. These can be seen from the mainland, most easily from the northern coast of the Snæfellsnes Peninsula east of Stykkishólmur.

Ísafjörður

This pleasant little town occupying one of the most dramatic settings anywhere in Iceland is the capital of the Westfjords. Set on a natural coastal spit in Skutulsfjörður and surrounded by vertiginous glacial walls, it can only be reached from the south via a single-lane road tunnel cut through the heart of the Breiðadalsheiðdi uplands that hem it in to the south. Inland from the spit is the Westfjords, one of the most sheltered natural harbours, and the approach to the tiny airfield across the town and close to the valley sides is one of the most exciting anywhere!

Hanseatic League traders used to live here in the 16th century, but they set up camp only in summer. The town was one of six that was given a licence following the abolition of the trade monopoly in 1786, and it developed thereafter.

Hæstikaupstaður at Aðelstræti 42 was built by the first commercial merchants in 1788 but Ísafjörður always made a living from the sea and things haven't really changed even today. Whaling was a major industry and the town has been at the centre of the decision to restart 'scientific' whaling in 2003 after a hiatus of over a decade.

The history of fishing is explored at the **Neðstikaupstaður** (Westfjords Heritage Museum), a complex of listed buildings and assorted fishing paraphernalia including several characterful wooden fishing boats. The main display is in Turnhús, an 18th-century warehouse.

The town has numerous pretty houses that date from the late 19th and early 20th century. Take the walk (*see pp88–9*) for some of the more picturesque examples.

There is a well-established ski station on the slopes above the town. Ísafjörður Ski Week, held over Easter, is the highlight of the winter season when competitions on the piste and arts exhibitions, musical performances and a party atmosphere invade the town.

Situated 4km north of the town, the village of **Hnífsdalur** is a centre of production for *hákarl* or putrid shark. Admittedly it is an acquired taste but you will find it nowhere else but in Iceland.

A trawler in Ísafjörður

Ólafsvík scenery

In addition to the route from the south Ísafjörður is linked to the outside world by route 61 leading east in and out of the sub-fjords that sprout from Ísafjörðardjúp, a wide exit to the Atlantic. It is a majestic landscape of wide glacial valleys punctuated by small farmsteads. At the outlet of Skötufjörður above the road is the turf farmhouse of **Litlbær**. Now owned by the National Museum of Iceland, this small collection of buildings from the late 1800s was home to two families until 1969.

Neðstikaupstaður: Suðurgata. Tel: 456 4418. Open: Jun–Aug Mon–Fri 10am–5pm, Sat–Sun 1–5pm. Admission charge.

Ólafsvík

Issued a trade licence in 1687, the old warehouse of **Gamla Pakkhúðið** harks back to an era of wealth; it was built in 1841 by the Clausen family, then the leading commercial entrepreneurs of the town. The building now houses the tourist office and the Snæfellsbaejar Regional Museum, with folklore galleries and artefacts of local life and lifestyle. There is also **Sjavarsafnið Ólafsvík**, a small maritime museum by the harbour.

Gamla Pakkhúðið: Ólafsbraut. Tel: 436 1543. Open: Jun–Aug 9am–7pm. Admission charge.
Sjavarsafnið Ólafsvík: Hafn. Tel: 436 6961. Open: Jun–Aug daily 10am–6pm. Admission charge.

Snæfellsjökull National Park

The archetypal volcanic cone of Snæfellsjökull (1446m) which can easily be seen from Reykjavik acts as a magnet attracting travellers north. The barely dormant volcano is shrouded in myth.

Columbus does his homework

It is believed that Christopher Columbus visited a previous church on the site of Ingjaldhóll in 1477 when he came to consult the *Sagas* about routes to west Vinland in preparation for his own epic voyage of discovery. A painting in the church depicts his meeting with the local clergymen but there is no record of whether he learned anything that proved to be of value to him when he sailed.

It was a totem to the Norsemen who thought it to be the home of trolls; is considered a powerful source of positive energy by 'new-agers'; and was the setting for Jules Verne's *Journey to the Centre of the Earth* where the explorers set out to the earth's belly by climbing down the volcano's 1km wide crater.

That the volcano was active till very recently (in geological time at least) is evidenced by the layers of petrified lava flowing from every face. The western faces look like the surface of the human brain with rivulets of molten rock that have hardened and rounded as they dried. Atop this is a gleaming white snow cap, one of Iceland's smallest but prettiest glaciers.

To the northwest of the peak itself, the lava flows stretch out across a sanður to the high black basalt cliffs at Öndverðarnes where a couple of lighthouses protect shipping from the treacherous waters. There are several walking routes around the pseudo-craters here or along the coast past the highest structure on the island, a 420m-long wave radio mast, to Hellissandur with Sjomannagarður, its small turf-roofed maritime museum (*on the main coast road, Hellissandur; tel: 436 6784; open: Jun–Aug Tue–Thur 10am–6pm; admission charge*). The church at Ingjaldhóll just beyond the town is said to be the oldest concrete church in Iceland, erected in 1903.

Snæfellsjökull glacier can be seen from Reykjavik, atop the dormant volcano

Boats moored at the harbour at Stykkishólmur

Strandir *(see p49, p79 & pp142–3)*

Stykkishólmur

A municipality only since 1987, Stykkishólmur is nonetheless the leading town on the Snæfellsnes. It is set on a short peninsula jutting into Breiðafjörður with panoramic sea views to the north.

The oldest building in the town Norska Húdið (Norwegian House) was imported from Bergen in 1832 by Árni Thorlacius, considered the 'father of Stykkishólmur'. It houses a collection of furniture and artefacts donated by or

rescued from local households. Árni used to take daily meteorological readings during his youth, a practice that continues to this day; these form an invaluable resource to metereological scientists. The ferry *Baldur* links

The Berserkers

The Berserkers were fanatical mercenaries, feared for their frenzied attacks and employed by rich Norsemen to do their dirty work. The name possibly comes from the Old Norse *bjorn serkr* or 'bear coat' which the warriors wore. Their behaviour gave us the modern word berserk – meaning 'out of control with anger or excitement'.

Stykkishólmur with the Westfjords in a three-hour trip, with a port of call at Flatay Island (*see pp78–9*).

Inland from the town is a small hill called **Helgafell** that was sacred to the people of the *Saga* era. It was the home of Snorri goði (the northern tribal chief in the *Eyrbyggja Saga*) and the final resting place of Guðrún Ósvifursdóttir (of the *Laxdæla Saga*).

15km west of Stykkishólmur lies the Berserkjahraun or Berserks lava field, scene of a famous incident in *Eyrbyggja Saga*. The farmer of Hraun returned from Norway with a couple of men. But they took a shine to his daughter. The farmer set them what he thought was an impossible task – to clear a path through the lava fields to his brother's farm – and offered his daughter's hand in marriage to the man who could do the job. The task was completed in record time, but the farmer reneged on his deal and his daughter married Snorri goði instead! *Norska Húdið. Hafnargata 5. Tel: 438 1640. Open: Jun–Aug daily 11am–5pm, by arrangement at other times. Admission charge.*

Getting Around
If you would rather let someone else take the driving strain, try the Snæfelljökull bus that does a complete lap of the western Snæfellsnes every weekday afternoon during the summer. You can buy a circuit ticket that allows you to get off one day and continue the journey the next; so you can enjoy a morning walk at Arnastapi, for instance. The bus leaves Hellissandur between Mondays and Fridays at 1pm.

Take beautiful photos while hiking in Snæfellsnes

Drive: Snæfellsnes Peninsula

The Snæfellsnes peninsula makes for an excellent day tour as most of the major attractions lie just a stone's throw away from the main route. It is also possible to do this tour in a day from Reykjavik – though you would need to get an early start.

Time: 8 hours.
Distance: 270km.

Start the journey at Stykkishólmur.

1 Helgafell

Leave the town heading south, past the sacred mound of Helgafell, until you reach the intersection of route 54 where you will turn left. Some of the road surface here is poor but it is the worst you will face on your trip.

2 Hvammsfjörður

As you travel along the route you will find outstanding views across Hvammsfjörður with its myriad tiny

Buðir church

islands. Look out for seals basking on the rocky shoreline.
Drive along the coast road with the waters on your left until you reach the junction of route 55 heading south to Borganes. Turn right here and the road climbs up the Heydalur into barren hinterland.

3 Oddastaðavatn and Hlíðarvatn

At the highest point on the cross-peninsula road lie the twin lakes of Oddastaðavatn and Hlíðarvatn, surrounded by an almost lunar landscape.

After the lakes the route drops through the vast lava fields of Koleinsstaðahreppur, to meet route 54 again.
Turn right. After 25km you will pass a right turn for Stykkishólmur. Ignore this and continue on. The road weaves across the coastal plain passing several lakes and offering tantalising glimpses of Snæfellsjökull up ahead. After a further 37km, route 54 turns inland to Ólafsvík and Hellissandur. Bear left on the 574 signposted Arnastapi. Watch out for another turning left to Buðir just a little further along.

4 Buðir church

Buðir church is reached by traversing the Buðahraun lava flow. Park here and walk the short way beyond the church and across the reddish sand dunes blanketed in tussock grasses to the beach, which is the finest on the peninsula.

Return to route 574 and turn left. Snæfellsjökull now looms ahead and you will see the route up to the mountain on your right after 12km. This road is not suitable for two-wheel-drive vehicles.

5 Snæfellsjökull

You can get close-up views of the snow cap and a chance to walk on the pumice slopes – rocks that were ejected when the volcano last blew its top.

Return to the 574, less than 1km ahead take the left turn to Arnastapi.

6 Arnastapi

Arnastapi is a diminutive rocky port set amidst amazing basalt rock formations – volcanic lava pounded by waves for millennia have created caves and stacks in abundance. You can almost touch the nesting sea birds here. The coastal walk west to Hellnar is worth it if you have the time (a couple of hours return trip).

The main road sweeps on in the shadow of the great crater. At the northwestern corner of the peninsula, the road doglegs inland across a flat plain punctuated by smaller pseudo-craters. As you reach the coast take the left turn.

7 Öndverðarnes

The cliffs around Öndverðarnes point are known as 'the black skies' in Icelandic, because they are so dark and foreboding. There have been many shipwrecks off this dramatically beguiling spot.

After Öndverðarnes, the road turns abruptly east to follow the northern coast. You will pass the towns of Hellissandur and Ólafsvík with their small museums before you leave Snæfellsjökull behind and verdant glacial valleys lead you back to Stykkishólmur.

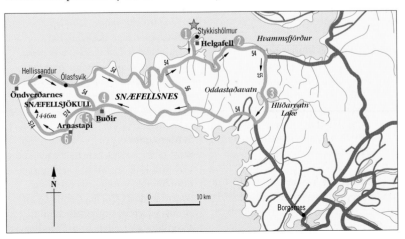

Walk: Ísafjörður

A trading port since the mid 16th century, Ísafjörður has a dramatic setting on a natural spit surrounded by the sheer walls of a glacial valley. It has been a seafaring town through the 20th century and is the administrative capital of the Westfjords. The compact town retains some interesting domestic architecture, much of which is still used as family homes.

Time: 1½ hours.

Distance: 1.5km.

Start at the whalebone arch at the main roundabout as you enter the town centre.

1 Whalebone arch

This arch is a testament to Ísafjörður's role as a Norwegian whaling station in the latter part of the 20th century. The town has courted some controversy since 2003 when the government voted to restart a small whaling programme. *Look north from the arch and across the street at the corner of the open green parkland is a bronze statue. Cross the street to reach it.*

2 Hafnarstræti Monument

This depiction of sturdy seamen toting barrels of salted fish pays tribute to the tough Ísafjörðurs who set sail into harsh waters. Many never came home. *Walk left from the monument along Hafnarstæti. Across the park to your right stands the Library.*

3 Hafnarstræti Library

The library is a fine neo-classical structure that also houses a small folklore museum.

Carry on along Hafnarstræti and turn right at the next intersection along Túngata.

4 Túngata

The mansions of Túngata that flank the park square form one of the most architecturally complete streets in Iceland. Though not the oldest in the town, they are copies of the catalogue houses brought by traders from Scandinavia, and are in good condition. *Walk along Túngata. Turn right along Eyrargata, then right again at Kirkjugata to complete the square. Turn left and walk past the church on the left to the roundabout and cross Sólgata to reach the oldest part of Ísafjörður. Take the first left, Hrannargata, then turn right along Fjardarstræti and right again into Managata.*

5 Managata

Most of the houses here date back to the 17th and 19th centuries. They range from humble wood-clad cottages to larger buildings like the Gamla Guest House, which was originally built to accommodate traders from Scandinavia.

Turn left where Managata meets Hafnarstræti and stay on this route (don't take the coast road). Turn left at Austurvegur, then right at Tangagata and right again to Silfurgata.

6 Silfurgata

Silfurgata has another ensemble of period properties. Though none stands out more than the rest, the depth and completeness of this district makes it one of few such left in Iceland.

The end of Silfurgata links with Hafnarstræti. Turn left here and continue past the post office. Hafnarstræti then becomes Aðalstræti, and where this road meets the coast road Póligata you will find the Tourist Office on your right.

7 Tourist Office

The Tourist Office is housed in probably the finest single building in Ísafjörður, a clapboard mansion and trading post built in 1781.

From the Tourist Office walk straight ahead into the warehouse area. The street is called Suðurgata but there are no signs. After 300m or so, the Westfjords Maritime Museum will come into view.

8 Westfjords Maritime Museum

This is one of the prime museums outside Reykjavik, important principally for its collection of historic buildings, the youngest of which dates from 1784.

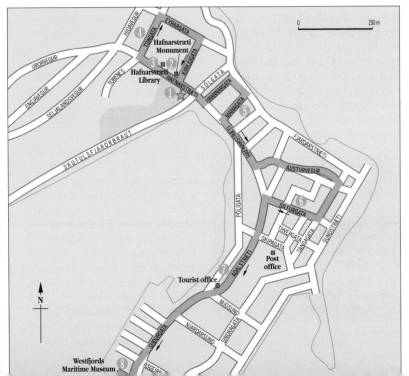

Northern Iceland

The attractions of Iceland's northern region are manifold. The major towns nestle on the banks of its rolling fjords while traditional farms sit square in the verdant meadowlands just in from the coast. Volcanic activity has given rise to some amazing natural features, while Captain Ahab would have been speechless at the sea mammal numbers offshore.

An example of architecture in Akureyri

Akureyri
Iceland's second city, Akureyri, is a worthy runner-up to Reyjkavik and the cultural capital of the north. The town sits at the head of Eyjafjöður and has a reputation for a mean *runtur* (*see p153*).

The town's arts scene is second only to Reykjavik's with a professional theatre company and a summer festival that runs throughout the summer. Exhibitions are centred in **Listafnið**, the town's Art Gallery, and **Listagil** (Arts Centre) that are located in the heart of town. Next to the Edda Hotel is a sculpture park with works by most of Iceland's major talents.

A street in Akureyri

The oldest part of the town is a 15 minute walk from the south of the town centre. The Main Street here (Aðalstræti) was the heart of the town a century ago and a series of clapboard houses still stand as testament. **Nonnihús** (Nonni's House) was the childhood home of Jón Sveinsson. The tiny wooden house, was built around 1850, is a typical dwelling of its type. It has manuscripts of Nonni's books and some of the author's personal artefacts. Outside the dwelling is his life-size statue.

Behind Nonni's House is **Akureyri Museum**, a rather nondescript building that houses a very good exhibition relating to the development of the town, with artefacts from the early settlement days to the 20th century.

Iðnaðarsafnið (Akureyri Industrial Museum) is the newest museum to be added to the fold. It concentrates on recent industrial successes. The regional airport also has a collection relating to 20th-century technological successes. **Flugsafn Íslands** (Icelandic Aviation Museum) charts the development of commercial flight in the country from the first takeoff in 1919 to the present day.

Northern Iceland

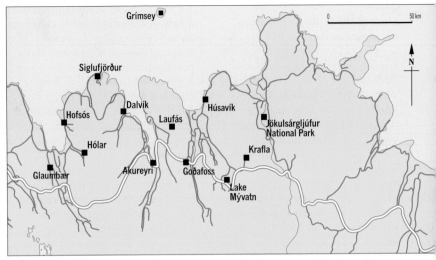

Around the bay on the road to Laufás (*see p100*) and Húsavík (*see pp96–7*) is **Safnasafnið**, one of the most innovative and proactive galleries in Iceland. Set in a large mansion, the exhibitions of works by artists and sculptors change every year but always include a rotating exhibition from the Icelandic Doll Museum.

Nonnihús: Aðalstræti 54. Tel: 462 3555. www.nonni.is. Open: Jun–Sept daily 10am–5pm, rest of the year by arrangement. Admission charge.

Akureyri Museum: Aðalstræti 58. Tel: 462 4162. www.akmus.is. Open: Jun–15 Sept daily 10am–5pm; Oct–May Sat 2–4pm, rest of the year by appointment. Admission charge.

Iðnaðarsafnið: off Droffníngarbraut. Tel: 897 0206 www.akureyri.is. Open: mid-Jun–Aug Mon–Fri 11am–6pm, Sat–Sun 11am–4pm; rest of the year by appointment. Admission charge.

Flugsafn Íslands: Akureyrarflugvelli.

Tel: 863 2835. Open: Jun–Aug Thur–Sat 2–5pm; Sept–May Sat 2–5pm. Admission charge.

Safnasafnið: Svalbarðsströnd. Tel: 461 4066. Open: early May–mid-Aug daily 10am–6pm; rest of the year for groups by arrangement. Admission charge.

Nonni

Nonni was born in 1857 and moved to the house in Akureyri when he was 8 years old, but after his father died in 1868 his mother was unable to cope with the household. A French nobleman offered to pay for the boy's education and Nonni went abroad in 1870. After finishing school he became a Jesuit priest and went on to higher levels of study in France, Denmark and England, and teaching in Catholic schools; he spent almost 20 years in Denmark. In 1912 he gave up teaching and began writing and lecturing. He wrote 12 books that have been translated into 30 languages, and delivered over 5,000 lectures. Nonni returned to Iceland in 1930 to celebrate the 1000-year anniversary of the Icelandic Alþing. He died in Cologne in 1944.

Dalvík

Much of Dalvík was destroyed in a devastating earthquake in 1934 so the town is not architecturally rich. But it certainly makes the most of its few claims to fame, the most impressive of which is that it was the birthplace of Jóhann Pétersson, also known as 'Jóhann the Giant', who was the second tallest man in the world during his lifetime, reaching 2.34m in his youth. He made a living in the circus away from his homeland but returned in 1982 to spend the last two years of his life here. Visit the town's **Byggðasafnið Hvoll á Dalvík** (Dalvík Folk Museum) to find more details of the man's life, including photographs and clothing. The other prominent display in this museum is the painting of a polar bear that has nothing to do with Iceland; however, the seal displayed with it was caught in fishing nets close by despite having been scientifically tagged just a month earlier almost a thousand miles away – that's pretty impressive speed!

Byggðasafnið Hvoll á Dalvík: Hvoll v/Karlsrauðatorg. Tel: 466 1497. Open: Jun–Sept 1 daily 11am–6pm, rest of the year by arrangement. Admission charge.

Glaumbær

This collection of 18th-and 19th-century farm buildings is one of the largest and best-preserved in Iceland, with an unusually long central corridor leading to nine rooms and a further four barns within the floor plan. Rooms 6 to 8 at the end of the corridor were the *báðstofa* or farmstead where the family ate and slept. It is said that these tiny rooms housed 22 people at one time. Each individual had his/her own cot-bed where a few personal belongings

18th and 19th century buildings of the Glaumbær Folk Museum

The Icelandic turf-roofed house

Glaumbær Folk Museum

were also kept, including an *askur* or wooden bowl in which meals were eaten. **Glaumbær** was a large farm with two guest rooms, one of which is the oldest section of the house dating to 1841, and a large pantry and kitchen. For most farmers this was an unheard-of luxury.

Apart from the sheer scale of the building, Glaumbær is wonderfully

decorated with the little nick-nacks, tools and valuables that a farmer's family would own. It is a very evocative collection and shows the creative capability of even the most humble Icelander, of men for carving and women for needlepoint and lace-making.

At the Glaumbær site, the **Áshús**, a clapboard house built in 1886, is open for sandwiches and snacks.
Glaumbær. Tel: 453 1673.
Open: Jun 1–Sept 20 daily 9am–6pm.
Admission charge.

The Turf-Roofed Farm

After the loss of much of their forests soon after settlement, Icelanders had to think carefully about what materials they could build their houses and farms with. The turf-style house, almost universal until the end of the 19th century, was made up of a thin layer of wood – often imported or even driftwood found along the coast – insulated and roofed by thick turf blocks that were held together by a living layer of grass. The roof slope was critical for the rainwater to drain away rather than soak into the soil. The farm was an interconnected maze of tiny rooms, often added to over time as the family expanded or when times were good.

The Icelandic Immigration Centre at Hofsós

Goðafoss

One of the most accessible major falls in Iceland, Goðafoss is only metres from the ring road, It is a cascade of brown frothy water heading seaward from the Ódáðahraun hills. The falls are the so-called 'Waterfall of the Gods' because after the lögsögumaður Þorgier went to a meeting to declare Iceland a monotheist Christian country, he threw his pagan statues into these waters on his return journey home.

Grímsey

The country's only territory within the Arctic Circle, Grímsey is 40km north of mainland Iceland. Most visitors venture here for birdwatching – the birdlife includes vast colonies of puffins, razorbills, guillemots and terns among others. The easiest way to reach Grímsey is by ferry from Akureyri.

Hofsós

One of Iceland's oldest trading ports, a cluster of 18th-century original and replica buildings sit on either side of the narrow coastal inlet overlooking the harbour at Hofsós. The setting, minus the clutter of modern intrusions, shows pretty much what one of these many trading centres would have looked like in its heyday.

On the south side is **Frændgarður**, an 18th-century warehouse that is architecturally valuable and owned by the National Museum of Iceland. Next door to this is a replica of the **Nýja Konungsverslunarhúsið** (The King's Retail Store) that stood here throughout the 19th century.

Head north (you will need to head inland and cross the modern bridge) to find a collection of trader buildings that host **Vesturfarasetrið** (the Icelandic

Immigration Centre). The exhibition 'The Road to Zion' tells the story of the trials and tribulations of the 19th-century Icelanders who abandoned their homesteads and headed across the Atlantic to join the community of the Church of Jesus Christ of Latter Day Saints. The red, white and blue **Gamla Kaupfélagið** (The Old Co-op) dating from 1909 concentrates on the lives of the Icelandic settlers who moved to make a fresh start in the 'New World'. The photographs might be the most interesting to non-Icelandic speakers.

The Centre also plays an integral part in genealogical research relating to the bloodline of Icelandic Americans and in forging links between the generations living on the island and in the US.

Just south of the town is a tiny turf **Gröf chapel**, thought to be the oldest in Iceland.

Vesturfarasetrið. Hofsós. Tel: 453 7935. Open: Jun 8–Sept 8 daily 11am–6pm, rest of the year by arrangement. Museum: admission charge; genealogy room: admission free.

Hólar

One of two Icelandic Bishoprics during the Catholic era, the present **Lutheran Cathedral** was finished in 1763 during the Bishopric of Gisli Magnússon in a late-Baroque style. The interior is rather plain but the earlier altarpiece (c1500) is wonderfully detailed with panels depicting scenes from the Bible. Several artefacts belong to Bishop Guðbrandur Þorláksson (bishop from 1571–1627), a forward-thinking man for his time, who was the first person to create a map of Iceland, for example.

His *Guðbrandsbiblia* was the first bible to be produced in the Icelandic language, in 1584. The portrait of the bishop is the oldest known portrait of an Icelander, painted in 1620.

Hólar Cathedral: open: daily 9am–6pm. Admission free.

The late-Baroque style Hólar Cathedral

Turf houses in Hólar

Húsavík

'European Capital of Whale Watching' is the town's self-appointed epithet and it is probably not far from the truth. The boats here can offer an over-96 per cent success rate because the town sits just below the busy seasonal migratory lanes that run through the nutrient-rich waters of the Arctic Circle, just north of town. Húsavík used to be a major harvester of the sea but today the poacher has turned gamekeeper, and whale-watching craft of various descriptions set sail morning and afternoon in season and weather permitting.

Hvalasafnið á Húsavík (the Húsavík Whale Museum) is an award-winning non-profit exhibition that speaks of all things whale-connected, from their gargantuan size (shown through skeletons) to their habits and intelligence, with interactive and technological displays and dioramas. Some of the most touching footage is of whale hunting and mass whale strandings, which have still to be fully explained. Anyone with an interest in the world's ocean ecosystems will find the place fascinating.

The town's **Byggðasafnið** (Folk Museum) has several sections including a good maritime display, a collection of over 35,000 photographs and the district archives. The Natural History section has a stuffed polar bear. This unfortunate animal met its end at Grímsey (*see p94*) in 1969 after drifting south from Greenland.

An other rather off-the-wall collection in the town is **Hið Íslenzka Reðasafn** (Icelandic Phallological Museum),

Húsavík harbour

Húsavík Whale Centre

A whale skeleton on display at the Whale Centre

where the pagan power of phallology is celebrated with a range of interesting representations. Look out also for the town church, which is a wonderful confection of gingerbread decoration built in 1907.

Hvalasafnið á Húsavík: Hafnarstétt. Tel: 464 2520. www.icewhale.is Open: Jun–Aug daily 9am–9pm; May & Sept 10am–5pm. Admission charge.

Hið Íslenzka Reðasafn: Héðinsbraut 3a. Tel: 561 6663. www.phallus.is Open: May 20–Sept10 daily noon–6pm. Admission charge. Byggðasafnið: Stóragarði 17. Tel: 464 1860. www.husmus.is. Open: Jun–Aug daily 10am–6pm; Sept–May Mon–Fri 9am–noon & 1–4pm. Admission charge.

Jökulsárgljúfur National Park

Also mentioned in 'Getting Away From It All' (*see p141*), Jökulsárgljúfur is at the same time one of the most visited places in Iceland and one of the least explored. Protecting the ruggedly beautiful gorge of the **Jökulsá á Fjöllum** River, the valley bottom remains a world apart; but its major cascade, Dettifoss is a magnet for independent travellers and tour groups, a thundering force of sedimentary dun-brown water from the central glaciers that drops 44m over a curtain of grey basalt.

To the north, the head of the gorge has shifted in geologically recent times, leaving a dry false gorge, **Ásbyrgi** where you can explore the flora and fauna that have colonised the valley floor in a series of marked footpaths.

Krafla volcano still has seismic activity in the area

Krafla

One of Iceland's most famous active volcanoes, Krafla is now also a centre of geothermal energy, harvesting the heat that nature offers. At the bottom of the hill is an active area of hotpot activity with boiling mud pools and smelly steam spouts. Head higher towards the **Krafla crater** and you will pass a geothermal power station started in 1974 but never completed because of seismic activity in the area. Carry on to reach the site of the mountain itself at 818m. There is a scientific station here that takes readings round the clock, so in principle if the road is open it is safe to visit. Just below the peak is the **Viti crater**, a sheer-sided hole with a pool of caustic liquid in its depths. There is a footpath up and around the crater's edge. A little further away from Krafla, a 15-minute walk from the car park, is the **Leirhnjúkur crater** past numerous hot vents. The bubbling mud tells you there is heat very close to the surface here, so stay on the well-trodden paths.

Lake Mývatn

Set at the heart of a volcanic and geothermal area and on the mid-

designated a protected breeding area in 1974 and some areas are off limits when the birds are nesting. Mývatn has wonderful landscapes and several volcanic features around its banks.

The most prominent of these is **Hverfell crater**. Over 400m high and 1km in diameter, it dominates the foreshore and is considered one of the best examples of a tephra crater anywhere in the world. The black ridges can be walked but stay on the trodden paths.

Just south of Hverfell is the **Dimmuborgir** lava field where the molten lava has cooled and solidified into tall pillars and surreal shapes including one named Kirkjan because it resembles a church.

Closer to the shoreline on the lake's southern edge is a small park of pseudo-craters, **Skutustaðir**, set around a tiny body of water, **Stakhölstjörn**. The footpath here is a great place from where to appreciate Mývatn's unique ecosystem and environment.

Mývatn's only village is tiny **Reykjahlí**. Take time to seek out the parish church that is surrounded by lava spewed in the dramatic eruption of the 1720s – the largest amount of lava ever emitted from one eruption as far as scientists can tell. The church is said to have been saved by the prayers of the local parishioners. The **Mývatn Geothermal Spa** close by, opened in 2004, is the most advanced in the country.

Mývatn Geothermal Spa: Jardbadsholar. Tel: 464 4411. www.naturebaths.com Open: Jun–Aug daily 9am–midnight; Sept–May Mon–Fri 5–11pm and Sat–Sun 11am–11pm. Admission charge.

Atlantic ridge surrounded by extensive lava fields, Lake Mývatn is one of the most unusual ecosystems in Iceland – a shallow nutrient-rich body of water that is one of the most important bird breeding regions in the northern hemisphere.

Every year thousands of birds settle here feeding on the algae that thrives in the warm water. Others compete with the char and trout for the millions of black flies whose presence often spoils the trip for humans – Mývatn means 'midge', so you know what to expect. The northwestern flank of the lake was

Laufás

A little out of the town but still part of the Akureyri Museum, Laufás is a good example of a turf farm set in a wonderful meadowland overlooking Ayjafjörður.

The farm is not as big as Glaumbær (*see pp92–3*) but has nine interconnecting chambers and two other buildings. At its maximum capacity it is considered to have housed 30 family and staff members. The farm site traces its heritage back to pagan times but the present structure dates from the 1850s to the 1880s, and has undergone an extensive renovation programme. The artefacts on display including work tools dating from around the turn of the 20th century.

Laufás. Tel: 463 3196. www.akmus.is Open: May 15–Sept 15 daily 10am–6pm. Admission charge.

Siglufjörður

Out on a limb with a single road in and out, at the very top end of Iceland, you may be tempted to leave Siglufjörður out of the itinerary. But this is more than just another small fishing town and you would be missing one of Iceland's most fascinating museums: **Síldarminjasafnið** (Herring Museum), centred on a turn-of-the-century herring salting factory called **Roaldsbrakki**, is where teams of herring salting girls would descend in the summer season to gut, salt and pack the fish in wooden barrels in preparation for shipping. At peak production in 1916, 10,000 barrels of herring were salted. The building remained in use until 1968.

The rooms upstairs are a treasure-trove of everyday detail, from 1950s' Hollywood pin-ups to hair rollers to nylon stockings drying over washing lines. Up to 50 girls and women shared the communal kitchen and dorm-style bedrooms, though they had little time for sleep as the season was short and the almost 24-hour daylight was used to full advantage.

The Herring Museum at Siglufjörður

Take a trip back in time at the Herring Museum

The ground floor of the 'brakki' was used as offices and the wages room is intact. The rest of the floor tells the story of herring in Iceland – of the good times when the herring arrived in their millions and the bad when they failed to arrive at all. Outside the building a herring boat stands in a faux harbour, as if just docking to land its catch. On Saturday afternoons from June to early August, salting demonstrations are held at tables in front of the 'brakki'.

Those with an engineering bent will enjoy the neighbouring herring processing shed that was purchased intact by the museum and which includes the coal and dust-fired drying machines and the presses that extracted herring oil.

The final building is the most recent addition and is an excellent reproduction of the old quayside complete with a genuine herring trawler and several smaller boats. There are wonderful photographs of Siglufjörður in its heyday.

Síldarminjasafnið: Hafn. Tel: 476 1604. www.siglo.is/herring. Open: mid-Jun–mid-Sept daily 1–5pm; rest of the year by arrangement. Admission charge.

The turf farm at Laufás

Place Names

Getting used to the pronunciation of place names is one of the most taxing jobs for a newly-arrived visitor. However, many of the towns and villages have very practical and historically relevant reasons for their names.

Let us start with the capital, Reykjavik. When the first settler Ingólfur Arnarson threw the wooden pillars that would be the foundation of his farmhouse into the sea and vowed to settle where they landed – a common Viking custom, he watched them float away around a headland and towards an area where smoke or steam was coming out of the ground. Ingólfur named his farm 'smoky/steamy inlet' or, in Icelandic, Reykjavik.

Most places, be they historic settler farms or more modern trader towns, were thus named for the geographical feature that defined their location. Many were named before a written language was introduced in Iceland, so the verbal connection to an actual landscape or to the people living in a place, such as 'past red crag peak and the deep inlet, just beyond X's farm', was the standard way to describe a place.

Remembering the meanings of some of these words will help you understand what sort of place you will find when you reach your destination.

Á – river
Alda – a ridge of many hills or peaks
Bær – farm or small settlement
Bakki – river bank
Brekka – slope or scree
Brú – bridge
Dalur – valley
Djúp – a long inlet cut in from the coast
Eiði – an isthmus
Ey – as the ending to a name means 'island' (plural eyjar)
Fell – hill
Fjall – mountain
Fjörður – broad inlet or fjord
Fljot – wide river
Foss – waterfall
Gil – gorge
Gja – fissure
Háls - ridge
Heiði – heath or moorland
Hlið - mountainside
Höfði – promontory
Höfn – harbour

Museum and road signs

Hóll – rounded hill (plural **hólar**)
Hólmur – small island or islet
Hraun – lava field
Hver – hot spring
Jökull – glacier
Jökulsá – glacial river
Kirkja – church
Klettur – cliff
Laug – warm spring
Múli – headland
Nes – headland or peninsula
Ós – estuary
Sandur – sands
Skagi – peninsula
Skard – mountain pass
Skógur – woodland or scrubland
Staður – parsonage
Stapi – crag

Tjörn – small lake
Vað – ford
Vatn – lake or water
Vegur – track
Vík – small inlet
Vellir – plains (**völlur** in the singular)
Vogur – inlet or creek

Lots of place names are simply a combination of descriptive words such as above. So Laugarbakki is 'the place of warm springs on the river bank', or Kirkjufell is 'the church on, or by, the hill'. Of course it gets a little hard to follow when it comes to Kirkjubæjarklauster or 'church, farm, cloister', but it is usually a simple 'where, why or who' as far as Icelandic place names are concerned.

Drive: West from Akureyri

This tour around the fjord west of Akureyri takes you through an expansive range of Iceland's attractions.

Time: 8 hours.

Distance: 360km.

1 Akureyri Museum

Akureyri has a number of museums and galleries to enjoy, the best of which is the Akureyri Museum.

Leave the town by the ring road route 1 north. Where this cuts inland after 12km, carry on along the fjordside road, route 82 to Dalvík.

2 The Dalvík Folk Museum

The Dalvík Folk Museum is a strange mixture of galleries celebrating local industries and local luminaries such as Jóhann the Giant, one of the tallest men ever to have lived.

Continue north along route 82. Just offshore, the island of Hrisey is always in view.

3 Hrisey

Hrisey, a tiny island set in the waters of the Eyjafjörður, is the largest offshore rock after Heimæy in the Westman Islands (*see p128*). The island has been inhabited since the early settlement days and is a quarantine station for incoming pets and livestock.

After 13km the road sweeps inland, and up and over the foothills of the Thverárjökull. It drops again to meet the eastern coast of Skagafjörður and you will reach the junction with route 76. Turn right here for the 25km road into Siglufjörður.

4 Siglufjörður

Siglufjörður's *pièce de résistance* is the Herring Experience, a fly-on-the-wall look at what made the town great: its annual herring harvest. We are not talking of dry statistics here but an exposition of how it really happened.

Return down route 76 and carry on past the junction with the 82. The road swings into Skagafjörður proper; after 35km you will find Hofsós on your left.

5 Hofsós

The harbour at Hofsós has one of the best collections of genuine and replica historic trader buildings in Iceland. Visit the Icelandic Immigration Centre if you want to know why so many people left the country for the New World and how many of them fared when they arrived. On the outskirts of the town (on the left as you leave) you will see tiny Gröf, the oldest extant church in the country.

Carry on south on route 76 for around 14km where you will spot a turning left to Hólar.

6 Hólar Cathedral

Hólar Cathedral was one of two Catholic Bishroprics before the Lutheran Reformation. The church building on the site today is more recent but it has an important altarpiece dating from the early 16th century, as well as an almost life-size statue of Christ on the cross that is said to cause Icelandic women to faint because the suffering on the face of Jesus seems so real.

Return to route 76 and turn left. At the junction of the 75 at the head of the fjord, turn right and keep the water on your right all the way to Sauðarkrokur.

7 Sauðarkrokur

Sauðarkrokur has a small municipal museum on the harbourfront, and a blacksmith's workshop that is still in its original condition.

Stay on route 75 south of Sauðarkrokur. After 18km you will come to Glaumbær.

8 Glaumbær

Glaumbær is the largest turf farmhouse complex on the island and adds a great deal to your understanding of how the majority of Icelanders lived until well into the 20th century.

From the museum carry on south until you reach route 1, then turn left to Akureyri. You will reach the town after passing through 90km of exceptional upland glacial landscape including the Öxnadalsheiði and Öxnadalur valleys.

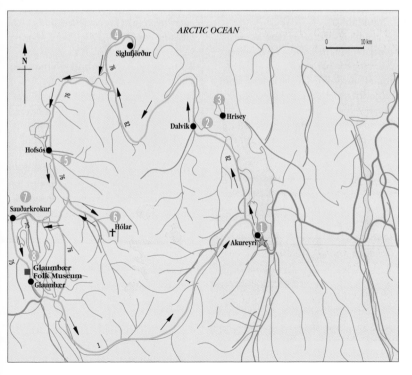

Drive: Around Lake Mývatn

Lake Mývatn is a unique ecosystem with its volcanic parentage and incredible birdlife. One thing you will need to worry about is the black fly, a main natural food source, that makes a beeline for your mouth and nostrils because it is attracted to the carbon dioxide you exhale. A handkerchief over the nose and mouth is useful but a head net is even better.

Time: 5 hours.

Distance: 40km.

Start at the main town of Reykjahlíð.

1 Reykjahlíð

Reykjahlíð is little more than a scattering of hotels and a fuel station, except for the parish church set on ground surrounded by lava flows from the devastating 1783 eruption. The church was miraculously spared.

Leave the town heading west on route 87 in the direction of Húsavík through the

Lake Mývatn abounds with birdlife

dark lava. After 4km turn left on route 848. At the junction is an information panel relating to the ecosystem and breeding grounds.

2 Hrauneyjartjarnir and Hölmatjörn

This route weaves in through the Hrauneyjartjarnir and Hölmatjörn lava fields where many of the fissures have cracked and dropped, leaving abundant holes and small caves now lined with moss that offer protected nesting ground for the birds. The waters of the lake are only a few metres to the east, so access is easy. Please note that this road may be closed during the nesting season.

After 11.5km the road crosses the Laxá River.

3 Laxá River

You will see many birds enjoying the oxygenated flowing waters of the river here, just after it has exited the lake. Laxá means salmon in Icelandic and these fish do spawn in the waters but only in the lower reaches closer to the sea. The upper reaches are prime trout country – an angler's delight.

200m beyond the bridge route 87 meets the junction with route 1. Turn left here to find the southern bank of the lake. After 5km you will find the Stutustaðir pseudo-crater park on the left. Stop here to take a stroll.

4 Stutustaðir

The Stutustaðir craters are small at around 20m in height. The collection lies scattered around Stakhólstjörn, a small pond now cut off from Mývatn proper.

Continue east along route 1. At Garður the road swings north and there are excellent views across the lake to the west here. After another 3km you will reach Hofði. Turn left into the small car park.

5 Hofði

Hofði is a beautiful wooded basalt promontory that offers some of the most picturesque views of Mývatn. The forest consists of a mixture of birch and spruce.

Continue north for another 3km to Dimmuborgir on the right.

6 Dimmuborgir

This lava field has some of the most intriguing and surreal lava pillars and cones, and features of lava fields usually found on ocean floors rather than on land.

Return to route 1 and continue north. After just over 1km you will see a farm gate on the right with a sign for Hverfjall crater. Enter the gate but remember to close it behind you as the area has livestock.

7 Hverfjall

Hverfjall crater is said to be the largest of its kind in the world, its walls built up by many small eruptions. You can walk up the sides of this 'black' hill but stay on the paths because this is a very fragile landscape.

Return to route 1 and turn right. After 5.5km you will find yourself back at Reykjahlið.

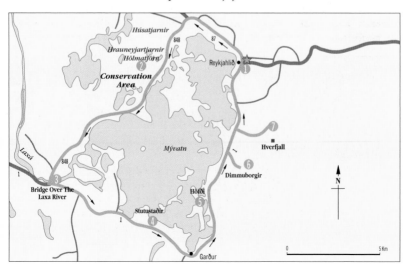

Iceland straddles the mid-Atlantic Ridge – a 16,000km seam in the earth where the North American and Eurasian tectonic plates meet. This area is one of the most volcanically active in the world, with an eruption every five years or so. **Mount Katla** has erupted 20 times since records began in 1104, and **Hekla** 18 times. Scientists estimate that around one-third of the basaltic lavas that have flowed since medieval times have been produced by Icelandic eruptions.

Most of the plate activity in Iceland takes place as seamounts under the sea surface. These are created as the plates move apart allowing hot molten rock or magma to reach the surface. However, volcanologists have concluded that in addition to plate activity, Iceland is also a location of hotspot (a very hot area under the earth's crust), further enhancing volcanic potency. This hotspot is thought to be small but very deep, extending up to 650km into the earth's core.

Types of Volcano

Volcanoes can be classed by the type of material that erupts.

Magma with low amounts of silica is called mafic. It is very fluid and travels

great distances. This type is more common in Iceland. Iceland's Þjórsárhraun mafic flow around 8000 years ago covered 800sq km and travelled a distance of 130km.

Magma that contains a high percentage of silica is known as felsic. It is viscous and solidifies quickly but can cause sudden explosive eruptions because it blocks magma chambers allowing pressure to rebuild inside the chamber. Mount St Helens in the USA is a good example of felsic activity.

Iceland has many other indications of volcanic or hotspot activity. The island experiences regular low-intensity earthquakes, has numerous natural hot springs (*see Spas p146 and The Green Issue p116 for further information*), fumaroles (from where hot sulphurous gasses escape from the earth's crust), boiling mud-pots (acidic hot springs coloured by melted mud) and geysers (superheated water forced through a narrow opening to explode into the air).

Icelandic Eruptions

1783 The largest lava flow yet recorded was at Laki when a row of craters spewed forth an estimated 3 cubic miles of molten rock. Livestock was poisoned by the gas and the sun was dulled by ash in the atmosphere resulting in a famine that killed 10,000 people.

1963 A submarine eruption on the Reykjanes Ridge off southwestern Iceland spawned the island of Surtsey. This virgin

land was thrust 130m up from the sea floor and had an area of almost 3sqkm.

1973 The volcanic site of Edfell on Heimæy appeared out of the blue. The eruption lasted for five months and was a classic sight, spewing molten lava and caustic ash. The lava threatened to cut off the town's harbour from the sea which was prevented by artificial cooling of the lava.

1996 The Grímsvötn volcano erupted underneath the Vatnajökull glacier, melting thousands of cubic metres of ice. This was released in a *Jökulhlaup* (catastrophic flood caused by the ice-wall giving way allowing a sudden release of melted water). 1.14km³ of water swept across the sondur carrying with it roads and bridges.

2000 Hekla: a 4.5km fissure sent ash several kilometres up into the air.

2004 Grímsvötn erupted once again with a steam plume rising several kilometres into the air.

Facing page above: cracked lava flow; below: Kerid explosion crater
This page above: Hverfjall volcanic crater

Eastern Iceland Coast and Highlands

Iceland's eastern fjords are totally different in geography from those in the west. With high slender peaks rather than plateau summits, the road hugs the water's edge at their base, and the several tiny settlements are strung along it like pearls on a string.

A sign outside a café in Fáskrúðsfjörður

In many ways, the towns of the Eastfjords take second place to their surrounding landscape and spectacular setting. Access routes up and over mountain passes offer panoramic views down the deep coastal inlets, while sea-level vantage points lead the eye to sweeping scree slopes and jagged peaks complemented colourful reflections in the languid waters.

Eastern Iceland Coast and Highlands

Fishing is king here, with every fjord having its own processing plant. The towns are also fiercely proud of their heritage and each has a small museum of some kind or another. If you are touring this area the linear route means you will be passing through most of them – so take your pick.

Djúpivogur

The oldest trading post in the region with a history dating back to the 16th century, Djúpivogur now has a population of just under 500 people. The cultural centre of the town is **Langabuð** (1790), once the town store and now a combined museum/gallery, information centre and café. Inside you will find examples of the exceptional work of the local woodcarver, **Ríkarður Jónsson** (*www.rikardssafn.is*), and a gallery dedicated to the local politician Eysteinn Jónsson.

From the harbour regular summer ferries run to Papey (Friar's) Island where

---

The creature of Lagarfljót

Just like Loch Ness in Scotland, Lagarfljót is said to have its own monster, Lagarfljótsormurinn. This huge marine creature is only rarely seen and has never been witnessed by scientists or recorded on sonar devices or video cameras.

the early Irish monk settlers founded a hermitage. Today it is a haven for hikers with a small wooden church and a lighthouse. You will have only nesting sea birds for company.

Langabuð Buð 1. Tel: 478 8220.
Open: Jun–Aug daily 10am–6pm.
Admission charge to museum.

Egilsstaðir

East Iceland's main town sits inland from the coast. There is little charm about the place itself but it is a base from which to explore the surrounding area and to take a boat trip on **Lagarfljót**, a substantial river that forms a long slim lake, **Lögurinn**, to the northwest of town.

Egilsstaðir's **Minjasafn Austurlands** heritage museum explains the history and development of the region and includes some interesting Viking jewellery and other pagan artefacts found at nearby Þórisá plus re-creations of rooms in a traditional farm.

The **Kárahnjúkar Dam** that will feed power to the aluminium smelting plant is currently being constructed inland from the head of the lake. The visitors' centre offers more information about the whole project.

Minjasafn Austurlands: Laufskógar 1.
Tel: 471 1412. www.minjasafn.is
Open: Jun–Aug daily 11am–5pm;
Sept–May Mon–Fri 1–5pm.
Admission charge.
Lake trip on Lagarfljótsormurinn cruise ship: from the bridge at Fellabær.
Tel: 471 2900. Times change with season.
Admission charge.
Kárahnjúkar Visitor Centre:
Végarður. Tel: 354 471 2044. Open: daily 9am–5pm. Admission free.

Eskifjörður

Set in its own inner fjord on the larger Reyðarfjörður, Eskifjörður plays host to the **Sjominjasafn Austurlands** (East Iceland's Maritime Museum). Set in an old warehouse, Gamla-Buð, dating from 1816, the museum showcases the importance of fishing to the region over the last two centuries, including details of the shark fishing and whaling industries. The old town's general store is also recreated here.

Sjominjasafn Austurlands:
Stradgata 39b. Tel: 476 1605.
Open: Jun–Aug 2–5pm;
by appointment rest of the year.
Admission charge.

The harbour at Djúpivogur

A small café in Fáskrúðsfjörður

Fáskrúðsfjörður

Fáskrúðsfjörður was settled by French sailors in the late 1800s when they used this fjord as a base for their fishing trips. The tiny museum **Fransmenn á Íslandi** (French Fisherman in Iceland), explores the history of the sailors until their final departure in 1914, from their fishing disasters to the close diplomatic relations that developed between the two countries. A small cemetery along the shoreline is the resting place for those who did not return to France. The street signs are in both Icelandic and French in remembrance of the town's foreign 'brothers'.
Fransmenn á Íslandi: Búðarvegur 8. Tel: 475 1525. Open: Jun–Aug 10am–5pm. Admission charge.

Hallormsstaður

Iceland's largest forest sits on the southern bank of the Lagarfljót close to Egilsstaðir. The 800-hectare tract was the private domain of Iceland's publishing magnate, Guðmundur Magnússon, in the 18th century. He began the planting of native deciduous species such as birch, ash and Alaskan poplar, a process that is now managed by the Iceland Forestry Commission. *Open access.*

Neskaupstaður

Home of one of Iceland's largest fish processing plants, **Neskaupstaður** benefited from the herring boom in the 1920s. The **Náttúrugripasanið** (Natural History Museum) does not have nearly as many examples of rocks and minerals as Steinasafn Petru (*see p115*) but **Tryggvasafn** (the Tryggvi Gallery) is worth a detour if you enjoy modern art. Local son Tryggvi Ólafsson is one of Iceland's leading lights.

Once again, it is probably the journey to the town, over the hills in the lee of **Mount Hólafjall** from Eskifjörður, that makes it worthwhile to go there.

Náttúrugripasanið: Miðstræti 1.
Tel: 477 1454. Open: Jun–Aug daily 2–5pm; by appointment rest of the year. Admission charge.
Tryggvasafn: Hafnarbraut 2.
Tel: 861 4747. Open: Jun–Aug daily 2pm–5pm; by appointment rest of the year. Admission charge.

Reyðarfjörður

Reyðarfjörður is one of eastern Iceland's newest settlements. It was not established until the 20th century but its sheltered position at the head of the longest fjord in the region brought it to notice during the Second World War when it played host to an important military base. British forces arrived in 1940 and a Norwegian air force squadron was billeted here in 1942.

Today the small and rather eclectic **Íslenska stríðsárasafnið** (Icelandic Wartime Museum) commemorates the war years. It is sited in the 1940s' Spítalakampur that was part of the original complex.

Inland from the head of Reyðarfjörður is the site of the new aluminium smelting plant that is due to open before 2010. It is likely to make the town one of the busiest and most prosperous along the coast.

Íslenska stríðsárasafnið: Spítalakampi.
Tel: 470 9095.
Open: Jun–Aug daily 1–6pm.
Admission charge.

Wartime Museum,
Reyðarfjörður

Seyðisfjörður

The cultural centre of the Eastfjords, Seyðisfjörður has a music school and welcomes many Icelandic artists during the summer. When the Smyril Lines ferry from Denmark docks it gets as busy as Reykjavik and this link ensures its economic buoyancy.

The town was founded in the early 18th century by Norwegian businessmen and developed on the back of herring fishing. As their wealth grew they began importing wooden 'kit' homes from Norway. At the end of the century Otto Wathne was the most prominent of these businessmen – he is known as the father of the town and his plant, Angró, was built in 1881.

In 1906, the fjord was chosen as the entry point for Iceland's submarine telephone cable – a new link with the outside world. The telegraph company brought new ideas and a new period of prosperity.

Today, Seyðisfjörður is one of the most architecturally interesting of Iceland's towns with a wealth of period buildings dating from the late 18th and early 19th centuries (*see Seyðisfjörður Walk pp118–19*), when the town was in its heyday.

Tækniminjasafn Austurlands

(Technology Museum of East Iceland) celebrates Wathne's legacy and the coming of telecommunications in a group of several buildings including machine shops that will interest anyone with an interest in engineering, the old telegraph station and the Wathne mansion built in 1894. Stop at the top of the one-way out road to Seyðisfjörður for exceptional panoramic views of the town hundreds of metres below at the head of its thread-like fjord.

A view of Seyðisfjörður with its lovely period buildings

Tækniminjasafn Austurlands:
Hafnargata 44. Tel: 471 596.
Open: Jun–15 Sept daily 11am–6pm.
Admission charge.

Stöðvarfjörður

This is home to one of Iceland's most
unusual museums, **Steinasafn Petru**, a
collection of thousands of rocks and
minerals collected over 70 years by a
local woman, Petra Sveinsdóttir. The
small house and garden are crammed
with examples small and large, and
include agates, zeolites and semi-
precious stones.
Steinasafn Petru: Sunnuhulið.
Tel: 475 8834. Open: 9am–7pm.
Admission charge.

Vopnafjörður

It is the ride into Vopnafjörður that is
the main attraction, though the setting

Seyðisfjörður church

of this small northern town is pretty
enough. Up and over the
Hauksstaðaheiði from Akureyri or along
the switchback incline of the mountains
to the south, the views are some of the
most dramatic in the Eastfjords.

Take the switchback for equally
impressive views over Héraðssandur,
the languid delta of the Jökulsá á Dal
and Lagerfljót Rivers, which is a major
birdwatching area. Just south of
Héraðssandur is a small inlet,
Borgarfjörður, where the artist Jóhannes
Kjarval spent his childhood and found
his inspiration. **Kyarvalsstofa** (the
Kjarval Experience) is this rural
community's tribute to their most
famous son. It displays some of his
works and acts as an education centre.

Inland from Vopnafjörður are old
turf-roofed farm buildings at **Burstarfell**,
which is open as a folklore museum
focusing on farm life from 1770–1966.
Burstarfell: Tel: 437 1466. Open: 15
Jun–15 Sept 10am–6pm. Admission charge.
Kyarvalsstofa: Borgarfirði Esyra.
Tel: 472 9950. Open: daily noon–6pm.
Admission charge.

to capture power directly from Mother Earth were as early as 1755, but a concerted attempt began in 1928 when the first boreholes were drilled to harness the hot water beneath Reykjavik. Today, 90 per cent of Iceland's houses have geothermal heat and you will never be short of hot water for your morning shower.

Iceland stands square at the heart of the green dilemma. It is one of the least polluted countries on earth and takes full advantage of what nature has provided. On the one hand it is feted as a forward-thinking example to the rest of the world, but it is also taking decisions that are unpopular with the international community.

THE PLUSES
Keeping Warm

Geothermal heat is one of Iceland's advantages. Inexpensive and reliable, it does not add to the world's problems of global warming or carbon dioxide emissions. The first attempts in Iceland

Ecotourism

Much of the appeal of Iceland stems from its natural abundance and the country has not been slow in seeing the economic possibilities, including whale-watching expeditions from around the island, puffin-spotting – though with two million birds around Iceland one would think you'd be falling over them in the streets, something that does happen when puffin chicks fledge and make an ungainly flight over nearby towns, glacier tours and volcano hikes. Hiking, cycling and horse riding are ecofriendly and popular ways of getting around.

THE MINUSES
Tin cans

Granting permission for the planning of a new aluminium smelting plant with a capacity of 295,000 tonnes per annum has become a national and international cause célèbre. Due to be online around 2010 at Reyðarfjörður (*see p113*),

it will have its own hydro plant by damming a major river valley, causing a major change in the landscape and ecosystem of one of the most remote and unspoilt parts of the country.

Polls conducted by the Institute of Social Sciences, University of Iceland, and the well-respected Gallup show that over 64 per cent of Icelanders approved of the plants. In Reykjavik fewer people were happy about it but in the countryside around 75 per cent said yes. The allure is the 1,200 jobs that the plants will create, in a part of the island that is losing people to migration because of lack of employment.

Whaling

In 2003, Iceland's government approved a plan to restart whale hunting after a hiatus of over a decade. Ironically, the country had come late to commercial whaling, leaving the trade to the Norwegians on Icelandic soil until late into the 20th century.

In 2004 the Minister for Fisheries, Arni Mathieson, said in a speech that since the country was 'overwhelmingly dependent on the utilisation of living marine resources', it would continue to kill whales for scientific purposes but that only the minke species would be involved – the take is well below that of other whaling nations including the US, Russia, Japan and Norway, and is said to be only 0.1 per cent of the total minke population in Icelandic waters. The research is said to focus on the role of whales in the marine ecosystem and to be economically sustainable because the whale products are sold in the world market – though only Japan has a demand for such products.

The website www.savingiceland.org has information on all areas of current environmental concern.

Facing page above: Entering the Krafla geothermal power plant; below: Reykjanis geothermal power plant
This page above: Geothermal power generation

Walk: Seyðisfjörður

Founded in the mid-19th century by Norwegian entrepreneurs, Seyðisfjörður soon became one of the most successful trading towns in Iceland. As the money rolled in these families began to live in beautiful houses, many of which were ordered from a catalogue and shipped from Scandinavia. Sixty such historic buildings have been identified; this walk will feature a few important examples.
Time: 2½ hours with museum visit. Distance:1.5km.

Start at the church on Bjólfsgata.

1 Bjólfsgata Church

The church was originally built further down the fjord but was blown off its foundations and rebuilt here in 1922.
Cross Bjólfsgata and walk down Norðgata.

2 Norðgata

The collection of buildings here make for an ensemble of Norwegian imports: the Framtið village store (1920), Lárahús built in 1899 by merchant Rolf Johansen, the Post Office (1903) and the 1901 Magasíníð used as a cobblers' workshop.
Turn right at the end of Norðgata and walk a short way along Vesturvegur; and look for number 7 on the left.

3 Vesturvegur – No.7

This is the oldest concrete building in the town, built in 1899 by saddler Böðvar Pálsson.
Return to the intersection with Norðgata, turn right and cross the Fjarðará River. Immediately on your right is Suðurgata. Stop at the first building on the right.

4 Suðurgata

Suðurgata was originally at the entrance of the drive to a hospital that was constructed in 1898. This first building on the right was the pharmacy. The Danish pharmacist also lived on site.
Return to the main road, Austurvegur, and turn right, keeping the fjord on your left. You will pass four colourful cottages on your left. Stop at Austurvegur 9.

5 Austurvegur 9 – Ós

Ós was the station house for the old ferry that used to take passengers across the head of the fjord before the bridge was built. The present house dates from 1907 and was built in the style of the imported Norwegian houses.
Continue along Austurvegur.

6 Steinholt

Standing alone on the right is Steinholt, built in 1907 by the widow Steinholt, it is the home of Seyðisfjörður, Iceland's renowned music school since 1976.
Austurvegur bears right once you have crossed the next intersection. Climb the slight incline to the first house on the right.

7 Einsdæmi

This is a corrugated iron-clad building from 1907, home of Iceland's first woman MP, Arnbjörg Sveinsdóttir. *Further up on the same side is Skaftafell.*

8 Skaftafell

Built in 1907 as a restaurant and guest house by goldsmith Bjarni Sigursson, the building also had his workshop and home. It is now the Seyðisfjörður's arts centre.

Continue along Austurvegur until you come to Fossgata on the right. Turn up here to Járnhúsið.

9 Járnhúsið

Járnhúsið was the first iron-framed

building in Iceland and part of a larger development by the Garðar company. *Return to Austurvegur and turn right. You will almost immediately come to the intersection with Hafnargata (Harbour Street). Turn right here and you will walk into what was the business end of town in the late 1880s. At the end of the town is the Technology Museum of East Iceland.*

10 Technology Museum of East Iceland

The museum comprises several buildings, including Otto Wathne's fish processing plant (1881) and the Wathne family mansion (1894), purchased by the Icelandic Telephone Company with the coming of the under-sea cable.

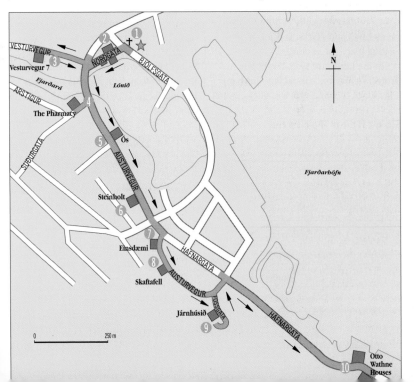

Southern Iceland

The south of the country is Iceland at its most intense, marked by brooding volcanoes, vast glaciers and a puffin bonanza every summer. Tour buses ply the route daily from Reykjavik but they only scratch the surface. The attractions here demand a stay of a few days, even if only to take in the sheer power of nature stored here.

A chalet in Vík

Dyrhólæy

This small wedge-shaped headland's name means 'doorway hill island', and it is taken from a stone arch protruding from its southern tip that is large enough for a sizeable boat to pass through. British trawlermen knew it as 'portland'. The cliffs around 'the doorway' rise vertically to 120m with many caves and stacks. It is a favourite nesting place for sea birds.

On the landward side, Dyrhólæy protects a shallow coastal lagoon that is a favourite roosting spot for eiders, swans and wading birds. The grassy slopes of the leeward side offers the perfect habitat for ground nesting species. So, all in all, this is one of the best sites for birdwatching. Not surprisingly, it has been designated a nature reserve. You can drive up to a couple of car parks to get excellent views of the cliffs from up close (if it's not the nesting season), or leave the car at the entrance and enjoy the walk (*see pp134–5*).
*Dyrhólæyjarferðir. Tel: 487 8500.
www.dyrholaey.com. Amphibious tours around the rocks at the site summer daily.*

Southern Iceland

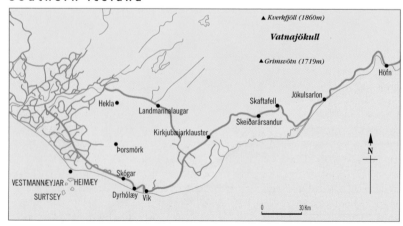

Dyrhólæy Lighthouse

Hekla

Brooding Hekla rises above the Vesturlandejar and Austurlandejar plains, casting a long shadow over southern Iceland. Her cold white mantle hides a molten heart and this volcano has been responsible for some of the most damaging eruptions in Iceland's recorded history including the most damaging one in 1104 that swallowed farms and villages within a radius of 50km. In popular myth, Hekla is the doorway to hell, a red-hot keyhole into everlasting agony. Her last gasp of hot breath was in 2000 so there is danger of eruption still, and a team of seismologists takes readings round the clock.

There is a small information centre on route 26 which adds both to the facts and to the myth.

Hekla Information Centre. Tel: 487 6587. Open: Jun–Aug 10am–6pm. Admission charge.

Höfn

Geographically, Höfn (pronounced like a shorted 'hope') is in eastern Iceland, but since its attractions relate to its proximity to the Vatnajökull volcano, it features in the southern Iceland section instead.

Until the building of the ring road, the town was as remote as you could get from Reykjavik as you had to travel west through Akureyri to reach the capital. That was because the Skeiðarársandur was impassable. Today, it is a sizeable if bland settlement, a commercial centre for the surrounding crofters and a commercial fishing port. Most visitors pass through for its range of eateries and for its **Ísland Jöklasýning** (Glacier Exhibition). Everything you need to know about glaciers – how they are formed, the effect they have on the landscape and the current state of health of glacial areas vis-à-vis global warming – can be found here. There is also an interesting video show about the last great Grimsvötn eruption and the effect that it had on the area. Many of the interesting glacial features along the ring road are signposted with the Glacier Exhibition logo.

Höfn has a couple of other museums that you can visit if the Glacier Exhibition has not filled you with an immediate desire to head out to Vatnajökull. **Gamla buð**, a mid-19th-century warehouse is the home of a folklore and culture collection, while **Pakkhusið** close to the harbour has a maritime collection and doubles as a gallery for local artisans.

Ísland Jöklasýning: Hafnarbraut 30. Tel: 478 2665. www.is-land.is Open: Jun daily 1–9pm; Jul–14 Aug 10am–1pm; 16 Aug–Sept 1–6pm; rest of the year Mon–Fri 1–6pm. Admission charge. Gamla buð: Hafnarbraut. Tel: 478 1833. Open: Jun–1 Sept daily 1–6pm. Admission charge. Pakkhusið. Krosseyjervegur: Tel: 478 1540. Open: Jun–Sept 1 daily 1–6pm. Admission charge.

Jökulsarlon

Another of nature's wonders, Jökulsarlon is one of the most

A boat trip in Jökulsarlon is a breathtaking experience

Jökulsarlon – an iceberg lake

Basalt blocks in Kirkugolf

photographed landscapes on Iceland and the venue (with computer enhancements) for the ice race scenes in James Bond's *Die Another Day*. Jökulsarlon is an iceberg lake and Breiðamerkurjokull's outlet to the sea.

Hundreds of these blue-white leviathans float silently in the limpid waters. In the distance beyond, the cold blue tongue of the glacier can be seen from the rocky shore and from the main coast road that crosses the lake's mouth. Boat trips head out through the icy maze for an intimate encounter that contains the secrets of millennia.

Boat trips: 20–30 mins from the car park at the site. Tel: 478 2222.
www.jokulsarlon.is
Rides from 10am–5pm depending on numbers. Admission charge.

Kirkjubæjarklauster

This almost unpronounceable name, meaning 'church, farm, convent,' is usually shortened to 'klauster'. The village sits on the southern borders of Skeiðarársandur. There is not much more here than a fuel station and hotel, though, as its name suggests, it was an important Catholic centre before the Reformation. Many of the surrounding hills and rock formations have names that hark back to the religious community that had a home here.

A couple of hundred metres out of the village you'll find **Kirkugolf** (church floor), a series of natural basalt columns whose ends have been worn away to resemble a manmade tiled floor, thought to be the remains of an old church.

Kirkugolf: open access. Admission free.

Enjoy a walk in the Skaftafell National Park

Landmannalaugar

Landmannalaugar sits in the heart of some of Iceland's most evocative landscapes – the red, gold and bronze hues of the rhyolite rocks that seem almost unreal in their intensity, especially when the sun is low in the sky shining its warmest light, geothermal pools, the highest geothermal field in the country, and upland valleys graced by lakes and streams.

The region around the lodge has some of the finest hiking and trekking routes in Iceland with some unforgettable views, but it is not the easiest place to reach and creature comforts, apart from the lodge mentioned above, are few and far between. If you don't have a booking to stay here, camping is your only other option.

Skaftafell

Skaftafell protects over 1700sq km of Iceland's most typical upland landscape, including a large section of southern Vatnajökull, the **Grimsvötn volcano** and **Mount Grimsfjall**. Much of this land is inaccessible but the southernmost strip, where glacier meets rock, is one of the most visited locations. It is famous for its majestic vistas and its many accessible walks.

Skaftafelljökull protrudes down close to the National Park office, and the rather untidy and dirty black tongue of the glacier sees an almost never-ending parade of visitors. The same is true of **Svartifoss** or Black Waterfall, named so not for the colour of the water but for the black basalt column that the cascade drops over. It is possible to walk down to the base and behind the water but most bus tour timetables don't give you enough time to do so.

Skaftafell is not just about the macro-landscape; it is as much about smaller elements such as species of flora that flourish because sheep and horses are not allowed to graze here. In summer there is a colourful population of butterflies and ground nesting birds.

Skaftafell was the site of a large farm and a regional Þing in the 13th century, located on the flat land at the base of the hills. However the encroaching Skeiðarársandur forced the farmer to rebuild 100m up the hill in the mid-19th century.

The National Park headquarters has lots of information about the flora and fauna, and access into the region. There are some excellent, well-marked walking routes up and beyond Svartifoss (*see pp132–3*).
National Park Headquarters: Tel: 478 1627. Open: Jun–mid-Sept 9am–10pm.

Skeiðarársandur

Iceland's largest glacial volcanic flood plain is also the world's largest – spreading southeast from the Vatnajökull basin to the Atlantic Ocean.

An ever-shifting carpet of meltwater streams and soft alluvial sediment, it has always been one of Iceland's most mysterious regions, little understood till the arrival of the science of volcanology.

Today, scientists can tell why the Skeiðarársandur looks like it does and how it was formed (by *jökulhlaup*, or a massive release of glacial meltwater due to volcanic eruption, *see pp10–11*), but cannot explain the strange beauty of the lifeless plain of gold and grey sand in the ever-changing colours of an Icelandic day.

It was common for Icelanders to gather stones to bring them good luck as they crossed the *sandur* and this tradition is continued here. When the road was built many piles of stones would have been destroyed but they were collected by the highways department staff and placed in one location around a small pseudo-crater called **Laufskálavarða** (between Klausters and Vík), the site of a farm destroyed in an eruption as early as 894. Place your own stone here and you would be adding your bit to this very Icelandic custom.

Look out also for a memorial to the 1996 jökulhlaup on the main road just before Skaftafell National Park.

Skaftafelljökull glacier is a majestic sight

The impressive cascade of the Skógafoss

Skógar

The first thing you will notice as you approach Skógar is Skógafoss. This 60m cascade is an impressive sight as it falls in a pure white curtain of foam; from either the summit or the base it is an excellent photo opportunity. Legend has it that there is treasure hidden behind the falls, but no one has found it yet.

The other reason to pull off the main road into the village is **Skógasafn** (Skógar Folk Museum). Like many of Iceland's museums, the impetus for this folk museum was provided by a single individual who wanted to preserve memories of the old ways of life in the region – though whether he imagined his collection would reach such epic proportions and constitute one of the best attractions on the island is open to question.

The farm at Skógar used to be the nucleus of the collection, set on the coastal plain nestled in the shadow of the Skógaheiði hills and within the soothing sound of Skógafoss. The collection of wood-framed turf and stone buildings dating from between 1830 and 1895, are equipped as though the farmer has simply gone out to the market for the morning and might return at any moment.

The museum expanded as the owner found many more buildings to rescue; he restored them and placed them behind the farm to create a sort of pseudo-village. There is a school built in 1901, a church – an amalgamation of several in the region, and Skál, a second farmhouse dating from the 1920s, all painstakingly returned to their original condition.

The collection of artefacts in the museum is almost beyond belief, and is displayed in a maze of rooms in the main building. Not a thing seems to have slipped through the net, from the finest house to the humblest shack – furniture, clothing, bedding and decorative items cram the galleries. Downstairs there is a natural history section with birds' eggs, butterflies and insects stuck with pins – a Victorian gentleman's dream. The museum's most prized possession is an 1855 open fishing boat, which was in use until just after the Second World War.

The final and most recent addition to the vast ensemble is a specialist transport and technology section charting the development from the era of one or two horse power (the four-legged type), to the arrival of motorised horsepower. Early snowploughs and attempts at amphibious craft look the strangest, and lorries, tractors and family cars show the development over the decades.

Skógasafn: Byggðasafnið í Skógum, Hvolsvöllur.
Tel: 487 8854. www.skogasafn.is
Open: Jun–Aug daily 9am–6.30pm; May & Sept 10am–5pm; Oct–Apr 11am–6pm. Admission charge.

The well-preserved Skógasafn

An old fishing boat exhibit at Skógasafn

Vatnajökull

Iceland's most celebrated glacier casts its eye over much of the eastern coast. A vast white cape with many smaller subsidiary ice flows (including Breiðamerkurjokull, the flow that feeds Jokulsarlon and Fjallsjokull), it rests upon one of the world's most active volcanoes, Grimsvötn, who makes its voice heard regularly, most recently in 2004.

It was meltwater from Vatnajökull that caused the latest *jökulhlaup* across Skeiðarársandur (*see pp132–3*) during the 1996 eruption – a scientist's dream but a road engineer's nightmare, as miles of black-topped two-lane surfaces were carried away into the icy seas by the sudden wall of water.

On a normal day Vatnajökull looks benign and you can get up close on a snowmobile or other types of glacier tours – trips take about three hours. *Vatnajökull Tours Hafnarbraut 15, Höfn. Tel: 478 1001. www.glacierjeeps.is*

Vestmannæyjar (The Westman Islands)

A collection of small islands off the south coast of Iceland, the Westman Islands became world famous during the volcanic eruption of 1973 (*see box*). Named so because in the 11th century they were home to a small group of renegade Irishmen or 'men from the west', only one of the group of 16 islands, Heimæy, is inhabited. Apart from its reputation

On January 23rd, 1973 in the middle of the night a violent volcanic eruption woke the people of these islands from their beds. Lava spewed from a new fissure, threatening their homes. Luckily, because of the bad weather that day the fishing fleet had not set sail from the harbour, and the 5,000 islanders were quickly evacuated by boat to the mainland.

The eruption continued and in March the magma threatened the harbour – the economic heart of the community. An emergency action plan to halt the flow by pumping millions of litres of icy seawater onto it worked well. All this happened under media spotlights as news crews around the world reported every twist and turn in the story.

By the end of the episode in early July, over 300 houses had been lost but the harbour was saved.

The Vatnajökull glacier rests on an active volcano

The volcanic sand beach

as a volcanic hotspot, life is quiet and uncomplicated here. The islanders make a living from the sea – the fish within it or the birds that fly above it, including millions of migratory birds that arrive to nest on the cliff of these islands. The economic harvest has always been in the meat and eggs of these birds, particularly puffins, which are considered a delicacy. Today, the traditional industries are supplemented by tourist dollars from whale and puffin watching.

The town has a handful of minor museums. **Byggðasafn** (Folk Museum) gives information about the island's history and development including a section on the eruption; **Landyst** is a small museum housed in the old maternity hospital in a fort built by the English in the 15th century. There is also a small **Fiska-og náttúrugripasafnið** (Aquarium and Natural History Museum) with a collection of Icelandic fish and dioramas with stuffed native animals.

But getting out on to the footpaths of the island is the real reason for being here. It is the best way to view the nest sites – the puffins spend time on land only to nest, so outside the June–September season don't expect to see anything but the odd feather or carcass. Another interesting trip is the route up the new volcanic cone **Edfell**.

Visit the island in season (mid-August) and you can take part in the puffin-chicks rescue programme.

A hillside farm near Vík

Thousands of fledging birds become disorientated by the lights of the town and fall ignominiously into the streets. Armed with a cardboard box and some soft fabric – a towel would do – you patrol the streets looking for them; carefully put them in the box and cover with the towel to keep them calm. The following morning the young birds are released onto the water to allow them to begin their journey to adulthood.

Westman Films run regular shows on the volcanic eruption, the birth of neighbouring Surtsey Island (*see p51*), whale watching and puffins, along with some interesting footage showing how egg collectors reap their harvest from the cliffs.
Byggðasafn: Ráðhústræti. Tel: 481 1194. Open: May 15–Sept 15 daily 11am–7pm; Sept 16–May 14 Sat–Sun 3–5pm.

Admission charge.
Fiska-og náttúrugripasafnið: Heiarvegur. Tel: 481 1997. Open: May–Sept 1 daily 11am–5pm; Sept 2–Apr 30 Sat–Sun 3–5pm. Admission charge.
Puffin and Whale Watching: Viking Tours. Hafn. Tel: 488 4884. www.boattours.is
Westman films: Heiðarvegur. Tel: 481 1045. Shows in English Jun 15–Aug 15 11am, 2pm, 3.30 & 9pm; May 15–Jun 14 3.30pm; Aug 16–Sept 15 11am & 3.30pm; 16–30 Sept 11am; rest of the year by request. Admission charge.

The Westmans can be reached by ferry from Þórlakshön (*Herjólfur; tel: 481 2800; www.herjolfur.is*), and by air on a scheduled flight by Íslandsflug from Reykjavik city airport (*tel: 570 8090; www.islandflug.is*) or by chartered summer flights from Selfoss or Bakki.

Vík (í Mýrdal)

Birds flock to the basalt cliffs around Vík í Mýrdal (always shortened to Vík) and now tourists follow, to enjoy the impressive offshore stacks and one of the finest black volcanic beaches anywhere. Offshore, the Reynisdrangar Needles have long been a navigation point on shipping charts.

Brydebuð, the old store, was built in the Westman Islands in 1831 and transported here in 1895. It is the oldest timber house in this part of Iceland and now hosts the tourist office and a small maritime museum. On the same street are a number of other gaily-painted houses and cottages.

Þorsmörk

Surrounded by no less than three glaciers, the high valley of Þorsmörk is a hidden world and can only be reached by a four-wheel-drive or special vehicle. The high Alpine scenery is worth the effort with numerous miniature canyons and cols (a saddle betwen two rocky ridges at the lowest point of a connection between two peaks), and fingers of ice extending down into the meltwater lake of Markarfljót. The ride across rivers and streams and past azure glacial lagoons is also pretty exciting.

Þorsmörk, meaning Þor's wood, is so named because the original settlers believed their God of War had a kind of holiday home here. Because of its pagan heritage, the valley is popular with Icelanders who come to spend long summer days and particularly the summer solstice, considered a magical time for the Norse. At times like this the hidden valley becomes the busiest place on earth – and the party goes on for days at a time.

The cliffs near Vík shelter numerous sea birds

Walk: Skaftafell National Park

Skaftafell National Park is most famous for its glaciers and volcanoes, but the southern tip has some wonderful verdant walking trails that head off into the wilderness. In this itinerary we have linked some of the park's easy-to-reach attractions, though we would still recommend hardy shoes because the paths are uneven in places.

Time: 3 hours. Distance: 6km.

Note: Refreshments are available at the café in Skaftafellsstofa, the National Park information building.

Start at the National Park information building. There is a large car parking area here.

1 National Park information building

The office has lots of information about the park's environment. You can get full scale maps for longer excursions and pick up souvenir books of the region – though it may be best to leave this for until after the walk since you don't want to carry too much weight.

Set out right from the information centre entrance and walk through the campsite along flat ground. Once past the site the ground rises rapidly. Follow signs for Svartifoss. The trails are well marked and obvious but the surface can be uneven with loose gravel, tree roots and small rocky outcrops. At the top of the crest you will head further inland to a junction of several routes. Once again follow signs for Svartifoss and as you continue to climb, the falls will come into view slightly to the left.

2 Svartifoss

Svartifoss is called 'Black Falls' because the cascade drops over a curtain of perfectly formed black basalt columns. The falls have a fringe of verdant plantlife, adding contrast to its dark walls. You can walk down the hill and across the stream to explore behind the cascade but beware of getting wet as the water and wind chill will leave you cold. *Return along the path you came until you reach a junction of footpaths. Follow arrows signposted Sel. Cross the small bridge and walk up the rise and through a small car park. Follow the road for a few hundred metres until you come to a right junction again marked Sel. Follow the signs and the well-marked path.*

3 Sel

The Sel turf and stone farmhouses mark the continuation of occupation in the region since the original settlement. Skaftafell farm was first founded on the plain but it was washed away by *jökulhlaup* and other volcanic activity and the domain was moved uphill. The ruins of the first farmhouse on site,

You can pick up information about the region at the Skaftafell National Park Information Centre

Gömlutún, can still be explored. Sel was built in 1912.

From Sel follow the footpath through the farmstead and climb to Hæðir.

4 Hæðir

Hæðir means 'high ground'. As you climb through the scrub and brushland (which includes harebells, yellow saxifrage and pyramidal saxifrage, the key Icelandic plant species), look south as the vast plains of Skeiðarársandur spread out before you. You will begin to see the many glacial creeks that drain to the sea. These change course regularly and are one of the reasons why the *sandur* was all but impassable until modern times.

Return from Hæðir past Sel to the junction and turn right.

5 Bölti

Bölti is the nearest working farm to the National Park and offers B&B

should you find yourself stuck for accommodation.

Continue down the road until it reaches the valley bottom, then pick up the footpath leading back to the Information centre, crossing the campsite once again.

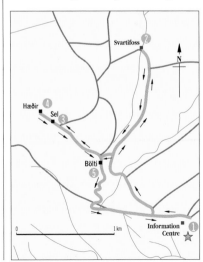

Walk: The Bird Sanctuary at Dyrhólæy

This small outcrop and its surrounding coastline have some of the best birdwatching conditions in the country. Dyrhólæy is a protected site and is off-limits at certain times of the year.

Time: 3 hours.

Distance: 6km.

Note: There are no refreshments here so carry water and a snack. There are cafés and shops in Vík, 10km east of the site.

The wedge-shaped headland is reached across a narrow isthmus. Leave your car at the small parking area just before the gate and off you go.

1 Coastal Shallows

As you walk you will see the ground of Dyrhólæy rising up in front of you with the lighthouse atop the site. To your left is a tranquil stretch of shallow seawater protected from the fetch by the rock itself. Here you can spot several species of waders, plus swans and groups of eiders foraging among the rocks.

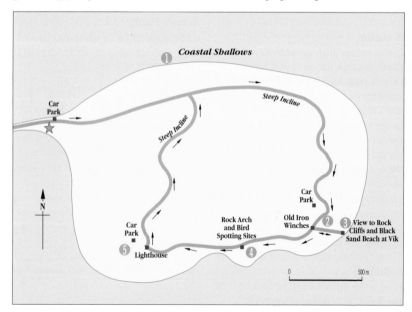

Continue to the end of the connecting spit where the road begins to climb. The track can be used by cars as there are car parks on the cliff-tops ahead. It is wide enough for several people to walk abreast, so you need not walk on the grass; but the surface can be slippery with loose stones so watch your footing. After a few hundred metres of climbing the road splits. Keep to the left and continue to climb. The track swings round with the curve of the cliff leading you to the car park in the southeastern flank. Climb the path to the lookout point.

2 Iron Winches

The remains of several powerful British forged iron winches indicate old industry at the site. Looking west you'll get your first glimpse of the rock feature that gives Dyrhólæy its name, 'doorway hill island'. The huge open arch below was carved by the power of the sea. It's now so large that tour boats travel under it with ease. *Turn left and walk for a few metres.*

3 Reynisdrangar Needles

From here there are impressive views east towards Vík, though the town itself is out of view, hidden behind the cliffs. There is a long black sand spit and the famous Reynisdrangar Needles, offshore basalt stacks, are easily visible on a good day. *From this vantage point set off walking west, past point 2 and along the well worn path across the cliff-tops.*

4 Cliff-tops

The sheer black cliffs of Dyrhólæy are ideal breeding sites for sea birds and you can spot their nests perched precariously on ledges.

Birdwatching in Dyrhólæy

Stay on the path and you will eventually reach the lighthouse on the southwestern tip of the cape.

5 Lighthouse

This is the highest spot on Dyrhólæy at 120m, and the southernmost cliff-top in Iceland – hence the perfect location for a warning beacon of light. From the cliff-tops look east to see the opposing face of the huge arch. Aesthetically, perhaps this is its better side.
From the lighthouse follow the track down past the grassland and you will see the shallows to the south come into view once again. The route is steep in parts here, so take care with your footing. Once at the junction, turn left and walk back to your starting point.

Fishing

It is difficult to overestimate the importance of fishing and fish products to Icelanders both as a provider of employment and economic well-being and as a filler of national coffers. Some say that the sea is in every Icelander's blood whether as an heir of the legacy of the exploring/invading Vikings or as a farmer of the sea. From its roots as a poor agricultural country at the end of the 1900s, it would be true to say that without fishing, Iceland would not be as wealthy as it is today. Fish and fish products make up 70 per cent of Iceland's export of goods today.

The island benefits from a shallow continental shelf and the Gulf Stream bringing warm water up from the Caribbean past the eastern coast of the US and the UK. This shelf is where the nutrients of the cold Arctic waters meet the warm current, and the fish love it!

Why

Iceland benefited from the development of salt processing in the early 19th century. This allowed fresh fish to be preserved so that they could reach distant markets. Fish freezing began in the 1930s and expanded rapidly; by 1950 it was a major component of the industry, a situation that continues to this day. Iceland has embraced the technological revolution in both fish harvesting and fish processing. Fresh fish in market stalls by the harbour is not the Icelandic way as it is in the Mediterranean basin. The plants here are state-of-the-art and the industry here is the most advanced in the world incorporating more freezing trawlers – ships that have freezing capability on board – than any other. This means that the fish can be processed and frozen even before they reach Iceland's shores.

Products

Sea fish, shrimp and other shellfish form the bulk of whole fish products.

The sea fish finds its way around the Mediterranean basin where it forms the staple of dishes such as *bacalao* in Portugal or France. Icelandic salmon, *lax* (salmon treated with black peppers) and salmon fillets tend to be sold in smoked or preserved form.

Dried fish and fish-heads make their way into fish-stock cubes. Fish oils have several uses: cod liver oil for human consumption and marine oils for industry. Fishmeal is a major component of animal feed or of natural fertilisers on farmland.

Major markets

Tonnes of fish are sold at auctions in Iceland's ports in pre-frozen state. Processed later in plants in the destination country, these could go anywhere in the world.

The salted fish, though declining in its share of overall percentage of production, is predominantly shipped to the Mediterranean coast where salted cod has for the last century or so been a traditional foodstuff and the base of many dishes. Iceland's salted cod can be found in fish markets from Portugal through France and Italy to Greece.

Fish meal from Iceland forms a major component in cattle-feeding programmes worldwide, while its fish oil still plays a role in keeping machinery working smoothly.

Facing page: Icelandic trawler
This page above: fisherman unloading;
right: cod in the fish market

Getting Away From It All

It is very easy to leave the world behind in Iceland. With a population density of 2.9 people per sq km and over a third of the total population living in Reykjavik, you need to travel less than half an hour outside the capital to be all alone. It follows, then, that this is one destination where you don't need to work hard or be addicted to 'extreme' sports to experience the wilderness, though you may still have to take 'roads less-travelled', pulling yourself away from route 1, the main ring road.

Hiking along the coast

We would not advise self-exploration far off the beaten track without a four-wheel-drive vehicle, a good map, warm clothing and back-up rations. In addition, a Global Positioning Satellite receiver, and a phone (though in remote areas there may be no signal) would be useful. We also advise that you tell someone of your travel plans so that in case of emergency an alarm can be raised for you.

If you are unsure of travelling on your own, resort to one of the regular summer tours that take the responsibility for getting you to the places you want to see. These usually cater to small specialist groups, so you will still feel like an intrepid individual rather than a faceless number.

Hiring a guide is a good idea – you don't need to be a group to do this and it can pay dividends in the quality of the experience you have, especially on the wilder walking and hiking routes.

THE CENTRAL HIGHLANDS

Iceland's central core – known as 'The Highlands' – is one of Europe's last great wildernesses. Off limits to all except those with special vehicles and Arctic experience in winter, it opens its door just a little in summer to let intrepid travellers take a peek. Much of the highlands are in fact featureless plains like the steppes of Mongolia, though remote volcanoes and glaciers add visual interest.

There are two main access points for vehicles travelling from Reykjavik. Each is given a route name and a road

The Central Highlands

number, and each has its own degree of difficulty plus its own attractions. The routes are not interconnected but the more difficult Sprengisandur route offers more interconnecting routes at its northern end.

The Kjölar Route

The most accessible is the Kjölar Route or route 35 heading northeast from above Gullfosss and cutting between the Langajökull and Hofsjökull glaciers to hit route 1 east of Blönduós. There is a bus service on this route in summer. The highlights of the trip include Hvaravellir with its geothermal fields renowned for their vivid colours; Hvítárvatn or the 'white river lake' with its iceberg decoration courtesy of Langajökull, and Kerlingarfjöll with its archetypal 'alpine' scenery.

The Sprengisandur Route

This route (F26) is famed for its vast sand deserts, monotonous to some but surreally inspiring to others. The route rises from the northern flank of Hekla (*see p121*) and travels between Hofsjökull and Vatnajökull (*see p128*) into the hinterland. It is taxing for vehicles and requires patience but once past the Nýldalur mountain hut it branches out offering several choices to the central northern coast and eastern Iceland.

Taking the easternmost route of these choices, the Gæsavatnnaleið Route, takes you to the spectacular Askja Caldera, with an interior area of 50sq km and the dark lake Öskjuvatn. The caldera was created in 1875 from a massive eruption that brought dark days to much of Europe. You will also

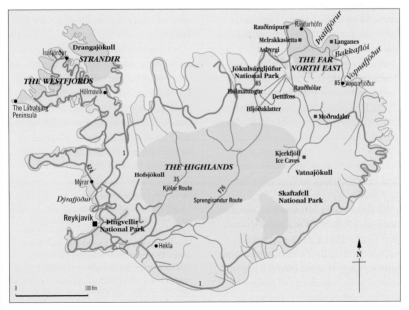

be able to visit Herðubreið, a sub-glacial volcano that has somehow lost its snowy cap, and the surrounding foreboding lava fields.

Kjerkfjöll Ice Caves

Another dramatic route runs south from route 1 just east of Möðrudalur. The Kjerkfjöll route leads eventually to a compact but fascinating area of natural wonders, the Kjerkfjöll Ice Caves. These caverns sit in an area of intense geothermal activity, and the heat and ice interact to create a vast and ever-changing ice sculpture interspersed with plumes of hot escaping steam – rather like where one might imagine Superman was born!

THE FAR NORTHEAST

Iceland's far northeastern corner does not have the dramatic natural attractions of the Central Highlands, however it is one of the least populated and least visited parts of Iceland, seemingly left behind as route 1 swings south.

You can access the route north out of the Jökulsárgljúfur National Park (*see next page*), where route 85 leads east around Melrakkaslétta into Þistilfjörur and then around onto the Langanes Peninsula before skirting Bakkaflói and heading south to Vopnafjörður (*see p115*).

Melrakkaslétta is the nearest point on mainland Iceland to the midnight sun and Raufarhöfn is its northernmost village. Its coastline is mostly low-lying, with numerous small inland lakes and coastal reefs, vast flocks of guillemot and kittiwakes, plus the spectacular

Hiking along a steep trail

Rauðinúpur cliffs, so called because the layers of iron oxide in the rocks are a vivid red.

At Langanes the road runs out two-thirds of the way along the peninsula, so a four-wheel-drive vehicle is advised, if only for comfort! The once-rich farmlands here have mostly been abandoned, and numerous buildings stand sentinel in the fields. The end of the peninsula is marked by yet another lighthouse, built in 1910.

And then there were two

Legend has it that catastrophe struck northern Melrakkaslétta when the plague wiped out the whole population except for one woman in the east and one man in the west. They met up at Meyjarþúfa (Virgin's Knoll), west of Raufarhöfn, and became mother and father to a whole new generation that repopulated the area.

JÖKULSÁRGLJÚFUR NATIONAL PARK

Already mentioned in the Northern Iceland section, Jökulsárgljúfur merits inclusion here because only a few of its many visitors venture away from Dettifoss, its major attraction and the 'Grand Canyon'-type panoramas from the major viewing points. There are also many interesting short day routes: through the abandoned gorge exit at Asbyrgi in the north (1hr round trip from the car park); to Hólmatungur (a 4hr hike from Dettifoss or by a four-wheel-drive vehicle) with its wonderful meadowland and waterfalls; to Hljóðaklatter or Echoing Rocks (1hr round trip from the car park), where the sound of the river is diverted through the gullies between the eroded basalt boulders; and to nearby Rauðhólar (2hr round trip from the car park), a series of small red volcanic craters.

The *pièce de résistance* is the two-day hike along the gorge rim from the base of Dettifoss to the mouth of the gorge at Asbyrgi. This route takes in many of the highlights above in addition to the aforementioned falls, and there is camping enroute. It is a popular trail so you won't be too far from human company – unlike the Strandir routes (*see following page*).

Tourists near a glacier in Jökulsárgljúfur

Water taxis in the Westfjords will take you around the region

THE WESTFJORDS REGION
Strandir

A world away from Iceland's 'fire and ice' image, Strandir is still one of the country's most magnificent regions. A rocky peninsula forming the northernmost section of the Westfjords, it is scarcely populated. Designated the Hornstrandir Nature Reserve and protected in the south by mighty Drangajökull, the park has no roads – just 500sq km of upland heath and tundra to explore.

Access is by boat from Ísafjörður (see pp80–81) or Holmavík (see p79) to several small coves with basic accommodation (it is essential to book these ahead of time) and eateries, or on foot from the tiny towns on its southwesterly and southeasterly flanks.

You can use the boats like water taxis to drop you off at several bays over a number of days, taking short hikes and returning to the same starting point. Or you can link several trails to turn a day or overnight expedition into one lasting several days. Remote abandoned homesteads, mewing birds, deserted hot springs and no sound but that of your own thoughts are some of the delights here. The Strandir is also one of the last refuges of the Arctic fox in Iceland and you may be lucky enough to see one on your trip.

A popular and relatively easy route is to take the boat from Ísafjörður to Sæból and then walk across Strandir peninsula to Hesteyri, where you will be picked up by boat the following day. Although this barely scratches the surface of what Strandir affords, it still offers some exceptional scenery.

Don't forget that for longer inland hikes you will need equipment, water and food – a night under the stars will be one of your most memorable ones on the island. If you would rather have things organised for you, several organisations run guided tours. *See the Sport and Leisure section (pp160–5).*

The Western Westfjords

The westernmost fjords of the Westfjords offer landscapes similar to Strandir with a few more creature comforts. Here it is possible to link short hikes with car journeys and to spend your nights in a comfortable bed.

The further west you travel, the more remote you get. Farmsteads drop in number, and vehicles too! At the head of every fjord are towering cliffs – some of

From distant shores
The island of Æðey just south of Strandir, the largest island in Ísafjarðardjúp, is now a nesting ground for eider ducks. In 1615 a Spanish boat was shipwrecked there and the sailors settled on the island. Local legend has it that they became aggressive towards the locals and local chieftain, Ari Magnússon, organised a posse, hunted them down and killed them all.

Take a trip on a whale-watching boat

Towering cliffs loom behind an isolated cottage

Iceland's finest bird-breeding locations – and the roads sweep from the waterside up and over the high plateaux in a series of breathtaking passes.

Help!
In 1947 the trawler *Dhoon* was shipwrecked off Látrabjarg and a dangerous rescue mission was mounted from Hvallátur with Icelanders scaling down the cliffs to pick up the exhausted seamen. When a film crew came to document the event they found another trawler in trouble in the same spot and managed to film the second rescue minute by minute.

This is the most westerly land in Europe and standing on the cliffs or at the water's edge you really feel a sense of wonder, a 'what's out there beyond the sea' kind of feeling.

The Látrabjarg Peninsula
The highlight of the southern peninsula are the cliffs around Látrabjarg in the southwestern corner: over 10km of towering rock reaching 400m in height that is prime sea bird nesting territory with all the major species found in one place. The locals have made a business

and it includes artefacts used by people living in the area over the last few generations plus, rather surprisingly, an aviation museum. The beaches on this peninsula are considered to be the best in Iceland, backed by cliffs or long spits protecting the coastal shallows.

Egils Ólafsson Folk Museum: Hnjótur. Tel: 456 1590. Open: daily 10am–6pm, but if closed the family at Hnjótur Farm can open it up for you. Admission charge.

The Þingeyri Region

Like stubby fingers, the outcrops around Þingeyri point northwestward towards Greenland. Route 60 cuts across the knuckles of this hand, taking most visitors with it fasttracking into Ísafjörður through the road tunnel, but the peninsulas here have some incredibly wild upland to explore including vast scree slopes.

Few roads cut into the heart of this region but the 624 leading from Mýrar on the north coast of Dýrarfjörður past Thverfell to Sæból makes a splendid if rough journey – on a clear day the views are majestic.

out of collecting eggs and chicks by scaling the cliff face by rope – not a task for the faint-hearted.

To reach the cliffs involves a long drive across Látraheiði where you will need to leave the car and set out on foot for the last few kilometres to reach the breeding grounds and magnificent views. At Hvallátur, on the same peninsula, is the westernmost home in Europe. East across the moors is Hnjótur, where you will find the little-visited **Egils Ólafsson Folk Museum.** Egils put the collection together himself

A four-by-four, essential for getting to some areas

Spas and Wellbeing

The lifespan of an average Icelander (81 years for men and 86 for women) is among the highest in the world. While many put this down to a shot of cod-liver oil with breakfast (you too can partake of this during your stay as they usually have bottles of the oil at your breakfast buffet – complete with its fishy taste and smell), there is no doubt that the thermal waters have a lot to do with the health of Icelanders.

Long before geothermal technology, Icelanders used the hot water generated by the country's volcanoes for everyday wellbeing – after all it was right on the doorstep and a great benefit in the cold winter weather. Hotpots (natural hot springs) were regularly used to warm cold bodies and over time they became meeting and socialising places – like the Brits developed the pub, Icelanders developed the hot spring. All communities, no matter

how scattered, will have a community hotpot and pool, and this is really the best way to break the ice – excuse the pun – with the locals.

Large hotpots, such as the one at Laugardalur in Reykjavik (*see p42*) consist of several small circular pools of differing temperatures. To get the maximum benefit it is sensible to spend several minutes in each of the

This page above:
Blue Lagoon thermal spa;
below: Nordica spa
Facing page above:
Nordica gym

pools, moving from the coolest to the warmest, before plunging into a temperate zone. This helps to liven blood circulation, promote muscle tone and keep the heart healthy. Community pots may have only one pool of constant heat but there is always a swimming pool close by for the contrast in temperature.

There are two major geothermal centres in Iceland. First, the Blue Lagoon, which is probably the country's most famous attraction; there is transport that takes you there directly from the airport so that you can begin the process of relaxing as soon as you arrive. The waters of the Blue Lagoon are full of beneficial elements, and the clay found here is said to remedy a whole list of ailments from arthritis to allergies. The beneficial properties have also been packaged in a range of skin and hair-care products that you can take home with you. Second, a brand new spa centre has opened at Lake Mývatn, taking advantage of the geothermal heat just beneath its surface.

Many pools also have saunas and steam rooms. Here swimwear is normally abandoned for bare skin, whatever your age – this is part of the relaxation process. A strategically placed towel is standard as you enter or leave but no-one is really concerned about the exposure.

You can spend time in the spa before your day starts – many communal pools open early – or to relax after a day's sightseeing. You will soon begin to feel the change: skin that is smooth and clear, and a body that feels more relaxed. Enjoy!

ETIQUETTE

Icelanders don't use hotpots to get clean. It is considered good manners to wash thoroughly with soap and water before entering a communal hotpot or pool area. And very poor form if you don't!

Shopping

Iceland offers some interesting and unusual souvenirs over and above the run-of-the-mill T-shirt or fridge magnet – though there is no shortage of kitsch cuddly puffins or models of whales in snowdomes. Well-designed and artisan-produced souvenirs form a large sector of the market, though prices are higher for these quality objects.

A clothing store

Clothing

There are some interesting options in clothing. The wool of Icelandic sheep has been used for centuries to produce warm sweaters and cardigans with traditional patterns and designs which can form the signature souvenir of your trip – and, of course, a very practical item for use during your stay. The very

A shop selling antiques

best are still hand-knitted but these are also correspondingly expensive.

If you prefer practical clothing but in more contemporary in style there are a couple of companies that make ideal garments for an outdoor lifestyle and for the unpredictable weather of the country. Try 66 North, Icewear or Cintamani.

Reykjavik plays host to some exceptional fashion designers, so if you want to wear something that isn't off the high street but has a great deal of style, try shopping here.

Natural products

Wool is one of the high-quality natural products found in Iceland. Others include horn, bone, stone and lavastone, which are turned into beautiful objects or carved into modern sculpture.

Art

If Icelanders are not making music, they tend to be making art – though more than a few can do both. The national psyche tends towards modernism rather than realism. There are always several gallery exhibitions in progress whatever time of year you visit, so make time to seek out that Salvador Dali to start or add to your collection. Glass and ceramics are also favourite media with Iceland's artists.

You will also find a range of excellent souvenir photograph collections to grace your coffee table and to recall your trip!

Jewellery

There are excellent jewellery designers across the island but most are found in the design district of Reykjavik (*see pp150–51*). For modern, one-of-a-kind pieces, it would be difficult to beat the choice here. Look for items using lavastone – a rock that is obviously very pertinent to the area – or reproductions of runic symbols and Viking designs.

Beauty products

The Blue Lagoon markets a range of facial and skincare products enhanced with the minerals found in the thermal pools that you can carry when you

Souvenir shop

return home. There is a shop at the Lagoon itself, in the same complex as the Reykjavik city tourist office, and in the airport departure lounge.

Woollen jumpers with a traditional Icelandic pattern for sale

Where to Shop

Reykjavik

For that unique design product, head to Laugavegur, the main shopping street, and Skólavörðustígur – an area known as the design district, where the shops are filled with crafts, jewellers and small clothing boutiques.

There are also two large American-style shopping malls filled with individual boutiques and more recognisable international brands. Both Kringlan and Smáralind are great places to shop, especially when the weather isn't behaving.

If you wish to bargain hunt, visit the atmospheric flea market where all Reykjavikians, from the trendiest to the most bohemian, head each weekend. Kolaportið, set in an old warehouse next to the Hafnarhús, sells second-hand clothing, china and collectibles, as well as cheap DVDs and CDs – though it is difficult to ensure the quality or authenticity of the recordings.

ER

Feminine design marks this pretty women's collection.
*Skólavörðustígur 3a.
Tel: 522 9955.*

Gullkúnst Helgu

Handmade gold and silver jewellery with lavastone, precious and semi-precious gems and stones.
Laugavegur 45. Tel: 561 6660. www.gullkunst.is

Kringlan shopping mall

TAX REFUND

If you spend more than ISK 4,000 in a tax-free, accredited shop during your stay in Iceland, you are entitled to a tax refund of 15 per cent of the price, provided the goods leave the country within three months of purchase.

Make sure that you get a Global Refund Cheque with your sales receipt, and that this is signed by the sales assistant.

If you are leaving via Keflavik Airport, and you are claiming back less than ISK 5,000, all you need to do is to take the Global Refund Cheques to the Landsbanki Islands desk in the transit hall on the upper floor, and you will receive a cash refund. There is also a kiosk in the same building as the Reykjavik tourist office. Alternatively, post your completed Global Refund Cheques and receive a refund on your credit card after about five weeks.

Iceland Design

Handmade glass and painted glass pieces for table and wall display.
Laugavegur 56. Tel: 511 3130.

Lara Gullsmiður

Handmade historical jewellery based on runes and Viking images, plus small ornaments.
Skólavörðustígur 10. Tel: 561 1300.

Mariella

Delicate jewellery pieces using precious metals and natural materials such as shells, coral, lava stone and horse hair.
Skólavörðustígur 12. Tel: 561 4500.

Path of Love

Designer Ragna Froda brings her unique style to a range of women's clothing.
Laugavegur 28. Tel: 564 6249.

Perlan

The Saga Museum has a wonderful range of souvenirs that are copies of genuine artefacts found in Viking sites around Scandinavia. These include jute and linen clothing, wool blankets, Celtic and Viking design jewellery, pottery and glasswear.
Perlan Öskjuhíð. Tel: 511 1517.
www.sagamuseum.is
Open: daily 10am–6pm.

Out of Reykjavik

Alafoss

A factory outlet store with a range of knitwear, plus a crafts centre and art gallery for one of-a-kind items.
Álafossvegur 23, 270 Mosfellsbæ.
Tel: 566 6303. www.alafoss.is

Souvenir stall

Goðafossmarkður

A cute little shop with a range of hand-produced knitwear and crafts that come from all around the island.
Fosshóli, 641 Húsavík. Tel: 464 3323.

Skaftafell Cultural Centre

This centre has a resident population of artists throughout the summer and holds numerous exhibitions. Works are for sale.
Austervegur 42, Seyðisfjörður.
Tel: 472 1632.

Skógar Boutique

This shop in the Skógar Museum has a good range of books, arts, woollen goods and handmade jewellery.
Byggðasafnið í Skógum, 861 Hvolsvöllur.
Tel: 487 8845. www.skogasafn.is

The Viking

Said to be the largest souvenir shop in Iceland, The Viking has a good selection of knitwear, crafts and T-shirts, plus some kitsch budget items.
Hafnarstræti 104 Akureyri. Tel: 461 5551.
www.thevikingstore.com

Entertainment

Coffee House Culture

The backbone of the daytime social scene is the coffee house. In a country that does not have a tradition of drinking alcohol (it was always difficult to get and is expensively taxed as a luxury item, coffee is the drink of choice. It is served in copious amounts – refills are almost always free – and is freshly ground.

The commercial coffee house is a place for people to meet and chat. There are always newspapers and magazines lying around, and some double up as galleries for art exhibitions or literary meetings. Many coffee houses also serve alcohol, blurring the boundaries between a café and bar. But a relaxed atmosphere is true of every one of these. They are great places to feel the pulse of the city.

Café Hressó

This Reykjavik landmark has just reopened under new management. You can enjoy board games with your coffee, so it is a great place for relaxing while waiting for that rainstorm to pass.
Austurstræti 20. Tel: 561 2240.

Mokka

An original Reykjavik coffee house, Mokka opened in 1958 and brought in the island's first espresso machine. Mokka is also famous for its hot chocolate and waffles. There are regular art exhibitions where you can buy the works on display.
Skólavörðustígur 3a.
Tel: 552 1174.

Café Oliver

The architect-designed Oliver is a smart, ultra-modern place for a caffeine break. Artist Alice Clarke was commissioned to produce the stunning wall mosaics. The café has a non-smoking floor throughout the day and early evening so you can escape the fumes here.
Laugavegur 20a. Tel: 552 2300.
www.cafeoliver.is

Café Paris

Opened in 1992, this is a major meeting place in the lower town with views out onto the main shopping street. There is an outside terrace in summer.
Austurstræti 14. Tel: 551 1020.

Nightlife

The club scene in the capital is one of the hottest in Europe, with the young and extremely fashionable population contributing to the vibrant air. Reykjavik has developed a unique entertainment venue – a combination café/bar/bistro that transforms itself into a cool club on weekend evenings. These are where you get to see Iceland's 'with it' generation and enjoy watching their seemingly effortless 'cool'.

BARS
Gaukur á Stöng

A legendary drinking venue and the only place in the city with live music every night – the music changes regularly, so check the programme for your favourite.
Tryggvagata 22. Tel: 551 1556.

Glaumbar

Classic sports bar with a big wall screen and over a dozen smaller screens scattered about the room. It becomes a nightclub late in the evening every weekend.

Tryggvagata 20. Tel: 552 6868.

Kaffisbrennslan

The largest variety of beer on the island is found here!

Pósthússtræti 9. Tel: 561 3600.

Kaffi Reykjavik

A little bit of everything, this place pulls people in for its buffet dinner (*see p172*); it is also a pub and has live music and dancing. Try the 'cool' ice-bar for a really chilling experience.

Vesturgata 2. Tel: 552 3030.
www.kaffireykjavik.is

Vínbarinn

The only dedicated wine bar in Iceland with a good range of reds and whites from around the world.

Kirkjutorg 4.
Tel: 552 4120.

The Runtur

The Saturday night 'pub' crawl in Reykjavik is so legendary it has its own name. Locals move from bar to bar and consume vast amounts of alcohol in a short space of time, so things can sometimes get a little silly and noisy – but generally people remain well-behaved.

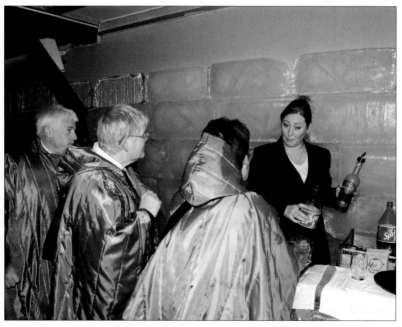

Reykjavik ice bar promises a chilling experience!

Young girl watching an event

NASA

A Reykjavik institution since it opened in 2001, NASA attracts a more mature clientele for its dance floor and its live music. Very popular and always crowded. *Austurvöllur. Tel: 511 1313. www.nasa.is*

Pravda

A long-standing feature of the nightlife, Pravda manages to stay near the top of the 'hotlist' and caters to many tastes since it has four separate areas with different types of music and atmospheres. *Austurstræti 22. Tel: 552 9222.*

Vegamót

This cool, funky neon-lit venue is another combination of bistro/bar/café and club. The clientele is young and cool. *Vegamótastigur. Tel: 511 3040.*

CLUBS
Kaffi Solon

At weekends this is a Reykjavik 'hot-spot' with a cool clientele and great DJs, but Solon is also a great café/bar and bistro during the week and is a must-visit place on the social scene. *Bankastræti 7a. Tel: 562 3232.*

Kapital

Kapital is a magnet for the young and trendy with the latest underground musical fashion on the turntables. It attracts guest DJs from around Europe. *Hafnarstræti 17. Tel: 511 7007.*

The Arts

With the emphasis on partying, one might be forgiven for thinking that the arts play little part in today's entertainment, but nothing could be farther from the truth. The arts scene is certainly alive and kicking, and Iceland has two professional theatre companies, which, given its small population base, is impressive.

Icelandic Opera

The Icelandic Opera has a short and

very popular season each year. For the rest of the year the venue plays host to a range of visiting domestic and international repertory theatre companies with lots of performances in English.
Ingólfsstræti. Tel: 511 4200.

Icelandic Symphony Orchestra
The professional company hosts a full and varied programme covering classical compositions and modern pieces. It usually performs in the Háskólabíð (University Cinema Auditorium).
Háskólabíð v/Hagatorg. Tel: 545 5200. www.sinfonia.is

Borgarleikhúsið
Home of the arts in the capital, the huge stage of the Borgarleikhúsið (City Theatre) is complemented by an intimate studio workspace. The theatre hosts a wide range of performances from avant-garde theatre to political debates. It is home to two companies, Reykjavik City Theatre, a 24-strong professional company offering at least six productions each year, and the Icelandic Dance Company.
Borgarleikhúsið. Listabraut 3. Tel: 568 5500.

Salurinn Concert Hall
Iceland's most technologically advanced performance venue with a programme from Vivaldi to Cole Porter.
Hamraborg 4–6, Kópavogur. Tel: 570 0440. www.salurinn.is

Out and About in Iceland
For a small and widely scattered population the rest of Iceland still has a vibrant artistic scene. Two high spots are Akureyri on the north and Seyðisfjörður in the east.

The Cultural Centre at Akureyri (*Listigil. Tel: 466 2609. www.listigil.is*) runs exhibitions and concerts throughout the summer in the annual

Façade of the Opera House

Reykjavik Dance Festival
The annual Reykjavik Dance Festival brings international troupes and choreographers to the island each September. Over 900 performances took place in 2004 in a programme that was incredibly diverse. Tickets and information at Borgarleikhúsið.

Festival of the Arts (*mid Jun–end Aug*). Performances run the gamut of visual art, music, theatre and literature. In winter, the Akureyri Drama Society (*Hafnarstræti 57. Tel: 462 1400. www.leikfelag.is*), Iceland's second professional company, stages four or five plays, to keep everyone entertained through the long and dark evenings.

Seyðisfjörður is the cultural centre of the Eastfjords and home to a concentrated population of Icelandic and foreign musicians and artists. Many artists from Reykjavik spend the summer here and the Skaftafell Cultural Centre

(*Austurvegur 42. Tel: 472 1632*) is where they hang out, holding exhibitions and animated debates. The Á Seyði music and arts summer festival takes place at venues around the town.

Art
Commercial Galleries
To complement the National Museum and the Reykjavik Art Museum, there are a collection of commercial galleries that hold regular exhibitions of native Icelandic as well as international works.

Turpentine Gallery (*Íngolfsstræti 5. Tel: 551 0707. www.turpentine.is*) and Gallery 101 (*Hverfisgata 10a*) are two of the best.

An Evening with the Vikings

The traditionally designed Viking Village at Hafnarfjöðdur offers the closest thing to a genuine Viking evening with a meal of Norse dishes served by staff in native dress plus some good old pagan singing and *saga* telling.

The Viking Village hosts a Viking festival every year in June where 21st-century Norsemen gather to celebrate the old ways, or stay in the Viking Rooms of the Viking Village Hotel. *Strandgata 55, Hafnarfjöðdur. Tel: 565 1213 www.vikingvillage.is*

The Hafnarhús Art Museum in Reykjavik

Cinema

Cinemas scattered around the island feed the demand for Hollywood all-star films; these are shown in English with Icelandic subtitles. There are several film festivals throughout the year featuring art-house and award-winning foreign language films, in addition to the highly regarded domestic products. One venue for these is the Háskólabíð (*see the Symphony Orchestra p155*).

Smárabíó (*Smáralind Shopping Centre. Tel: 591 5200. www.smarabio.is*) and Sambíólin (*Kringlan Shopping Centre. Tel: 588 0800. www.sambio.is*) both have multiscreen complexes.

One thing to remember is that most Icelandic cinemas still have an intermission. This used to be because the film reels needed to be changed but today it is probably more to allow smokers to have a quick cigarette.

Finger on the Pulse

For an up-to-date and somewhat irreverent view of what's happening in Iceland today, pick up a copy of *Grapevine Magazine*, printed in English. It is available free in cafés, galleries and tourist offices.
Grapevine also has an information centre at Laugavegur 11.

Reykjavik Culture Night

Held every year on the third weekend in August, Reykjavik Culture Night is the biggest such festival in the year with exhibitions, street parades, open-air theatre and fireworks displays. All the major museums, galleries, shops and churches are open late and there are events such as re-enactment of a pagan wake, Race of the Waiters (complete with tray and open bottle of wine), live accordion recitals and musical chess. The streets are packed!

Children singing at the cultural night

Young girl on roller skates

Children

Iceland is the kind of place you would love to bring up kids, with little concern about security. Though there are few specific attractions for children, there is plenty to keep them occupied.

Animal Magic
Free Willy?

The high success rate of whale-watching trips make it a sure-fire way of enthralling children of all ages. Birdwatching trips to islands like Flatay or Grímsey will thrill budding ornithologists, and spotting birds from land can also be rewarding though some remote cliff sites mean a long walk – the southern Snæfellsnes Peninsula and the cliffs around Vík are easily reached breeding sites.

Boarding for whale watching

Horse riding

The Icelandic horse is an ideal size for youngsters. It has adult horse sense in its diminutive body, so is not overwhelming for beginners or nervous riders. There is an excellent network of riding centres and stables all across the island, and kids can take instruction or head out on a guided trek on routes that suit the rider's ability. This is a great way to meet other children and make new friends.

The zoo

It is more of a petting farm and educational centre, but for most under-10s there is certainly a morning's worth of entertainment here. Lambs, kids and piglets are born every year, so the livestock is entertaining – the same goes for cygnets and ducklings. There are feeding and petting sessions throughout the day, plus a playground with slides and climbing frames.

Natural delights

Children are fascinated by the geothermic activity that is ever-present around the island. Strukkur geyser is the most famous and reliable, so that is a must-see, but the stinky steam plumes, hot springs and bubbling mud pools are equally fascinating, especially to older children. Keep small fingers out of hot pools even if silly adults around may not be setting a good example.

Sports and Leisure
Swimming pools
Almost every settlement – no matter how small – has a communal pool and these are usually heated, so they are comfortable throughout the year. For water babies, this is a dream come true, and another great place to make friends with Icelandic children who are introduced to the pools in their first few months. The most famous natural pool, the Blue Lagoon, makes children very welcome.

Organised Activities
Older children who like activity will have a great time in Iceland. There are many exhilarating outdoor pursuits to enjoy and the professional attitude of the support staff makes Iceland one of the safest places to have a go at something a little daring, including kayaking, Quad biking and on-and-off-road cycling.

The walking and hiking here is fantastic and there are routes for all levels of fitness.

Be aware
It is wise to remember that although temperatures may not rise very high in Iceland, the sun is still strong. So it is important to make sure you keep children well topped-up with a high-factor sun cream.

Children fishing at a jetty

Sport and Leisure

A trip to Iceland is as much about 'what to do' as 'what to see'. The phrase 'the great outdoors' could have been coined specifically for this island where the geography seems to have been designed to cater to the needs of the active sports person. Even if you don't normally enjoy physical activity, the landscapes are so beguiling that they invite you to join them and your outdoor pursuits can be as gentle as you like.

Cyclist taking a break

Angling

You will find some of the richest salmon rivers fed by glacial meltwaters here but Iceland has many freshwater species as well. The salmon season runs from June 20th to mid-September, while the trout season is longer, starting in late April. Fishing licences can be expensive but the rivers are carefully managed so a quality experience is assured. For something a little different, try ice-fishing in the depths of winter.

Icelandic Fly Fishing Service (*Storholt 16, 603 Akureyri; tel: 461 2456;*

www.tiffs.is) holds the rights to several northern trout rivers, and has access to salmon and char sites.

ATV Tours

For a little more speed and adrenalin, try heading out into the wilderness in an all-terrain vehicle. Once you have got to grips with the controls, you can don your helmet and go into the great outdoors following trails and traversing streams, accompanied by an experienced back-up team.

In summer, take control of a four-wheel-drive bike, and in winter get behind the handlebars of a snowmobile. Destination Iceland (*www.dice.is*) has tours all year round; contact the tourist office for other organisations.

Birdwatching *(see pp168–9)*

Cycling

Iceland offers good cycling trails for beginners, and challenging routes for the fit and experienced. Reykjavik harbour has a cycle path and the fjord floors around the East and West

Cyclists touring the fjords

fjords offer easy and picturesque possibilities.

Iceland Travel Ltd (*Lágmúli 4; tel: 585 4000; www.urlutsyn.is*) offers guided cycle tours around the capital and Blue Biking (*Stekkjarvammur 60, 220 Hafnarfjörður; tel: 565 2089 www.simnet.is/bluebiking*) has tours around the region. Bike rental from *Borgarhjol, Hverfisgata 50. Tel: 551 5653.*

Glacier Tours and Snowmobiling

Heading out onto a glacier is a must-do activity and you can either do this in the relative comfort of a specially modified Arctic truck or drive yourself on a snowmobile as part of a safari tour to feel the real power of raw nature. Warm clothing is definitely required!
Ice and Adventure (*Jöklasel, Hafnarbraut*

15, 780 Höfn; tel: 478 1000; www.glacierjeeps.is) run safaris on Vatnajökull throughout the year.

Jeep Safaris

The jeep is the perfect way to enjoy the excitement of the Icelandic countryside. These chunky vehicles with their huge tyres are perfectly designed for the challenging terrain. Most tours last a full day, but you can also take jeep treks.

Mountaineers of Iceland (*Síðumúli 8, Reykjavik; tel: 581 3800; www.mountaineers.is*) offers tours of the eastern island from the capital and Highland Expedition Tours (*Hrísateigur 5, 641 Húsavík; tel: 464 3940; www.fjallasyn.is*) runs tours to Lake Mývatn and the Jökulsárgljúfur region from the north.

Quad bike safari

Golf

Golf is a growing sport in Iceland and most small towns have set aside land for a 9 or 18-hole course that is a public access facility, with almost 50 in total. Don't forget that in the summer you can play almost 24 hours a day. The Arctic Open tournament is held in the course at Akureyri on midsummer night with the players teeing off at midnight!
Visit www.golf.is for more information.

Hiking

Walking and hiking is perhaps the major pastime for visitors and locals alike. You don't need to be especially fit to enjoy some of Iceland's most impressive landscapes, but comfortable, strong shoes and warm, waterproof clothing are essential.

The National Parks at Þingvellir and Skaftafell are perfect places to start, with easy and well-signposted routes. The birdwatching cliffs of the southern Snæfellsnes Peninsula have flat routes running by dramatic seascapes. Every area has walking routes that you can enjoy. Simply head to the tourist office for route maps or buy the more detailed Landmælinger Íslands maps (1:100,000 scale) from bookshops or the city tourist office in Reykjavik.

For more serious hikers, Iceland offers some very demanding routes. The trail along the base of the Jökulsárgljúfur canyon in the north is one, or the totally unsupported routes of the Hornstrandir Nature Reserve on the Strandir Peninsula in the northwest. If you intend to take a long or remote route, do

During the summer, golf can be played nearly 24 hours a day!

Trotting along on horseback to view the countryside

leave a note with your plans and timescale at your hotel. You will need food supplies and high-quality safety equipment to minimise the risk. There are around 70 mountain cabins that offer basic accommodation for 6 to over 80 people.

Icelandic Mountain Club (*Mörkin 6, 108 Reykjavik; tel: 581 1700*) and Icelandic Mountain Guides (*Vagnhöfði 7b, 110 Reykjavik; tel: 587 9999; www.mountainguide.is*) offer guided walks ranging from easy to difficult, including glacier hikes, and can tailormake trips for small groups.

Horse Riding

Viewing the countryside on horseback is one of the best ways to enjoy Iceland, and you will find stables all around the country. You will need a little instruction to master the technique required for the shorter Icelandic horses (*see pp166–7*) even if you are already experienced, but once you have gained the confidence there are numerous bridle paths to explore. You can simply hire a horse for a couple of hours to take a short guided trip, or take a day tour with lunch included, or decide to enjoy the whole of your holiday on horseback on long-distance treks.

Close to the capital, Ís Hestar (*Sörlaskeið 26, 220 Hardnarfjörður; tel: 555 7000; www.ishestar.is*) runs riding tours from their base close to Mount Helgafell including treks around the Blue Lagoon, Gullfoss and Geysir with pick-ups from Reykjavik hotels all year round.

There are bicycle trails for adventure-lovers

Out in the island, Eldhestar – Volcano Horses (*Vellir, Ölfusi, 810 Hveragarði; tel: 483 4884; www.eldestar.is*) offers a full range of day tours and longer treks. They can organise your whole itinerary and are open all year round.

Kayaking

The sheltered waters of the fjords are dramatic places to try sea kayaking for the first time, while the lakes and lower reaches of the rivers offer perfect inland conditions. From a kayak you can get a bird's-eye view of the migrating and native gulls, explore coastal caves and inlets, or stop on the river bank miles away from anywhere to enjoy a rudimentary picnic in the silence.

In the capital, Ultima Thule Expeditions (*Bíldshöðði 16; tel: 567 8978; www.ute.is*) runs guided tours. Another good outfit is Seatours (*Smiðjustígur 3, Stykkishólmur; tel: 438 1450; www.seatours.is*) on the Snæfellsness Peninsula, which does

morning or afternoon tours with a guide and equipment.

Skiing

Though by no means as challenging as the European Alps or the North American Rockies, Iceland has a number of small ski stations. Because of the long winter days, the runs tend to be illuminated, adding an extra touch of fun to the experience.

Close to the capital, the Bláfjöll ski centre (*www.skidasvaedi.is*) has 11 lifts with runs up to 10km in length and there are daily buses from Reykjavik when the runs are open. You can hire equipment and get instruction here. There are other multiple-run centres at Akureyri, Dalvik, Eskifjörður, Hengilssæði, Ísafjörður, Siglufjörður and Skálafell.

For more drama, From Coast to Coast (*tel: 894 0894; www.hofsnes.com*) offers skiing tours of the impressive Vatnajökull glacier.

Whale Watching

Húsavík styles itself the 'Whale-watching capital of the world' and it is true that the icy corridors of water directly north of the town are the equivalent of a motorway for whale traffic with over a quarter of the world's species passing through. Most whale-watching boat owners are so confident that you will spot at least one of these massive creatures that you get a free trip if you don't!

However, you don't have to travel all the way to the north of Iceland to go whale watching. There are good trips directly from Reykjavik harbour with an equally impressive success rate, and many operators in the smaller western and northern Iceland towns also.

Gentle Giants (*at the Harbour PO Box 720, Húsavík; tel: 464 1500; www.gentlegiants.is*) is a well established company who operates daily, weather permitting.

Seatours (*Ólafsvík but book at the harbour at Stykkishólmur; tel: 438 1450; www.seatours.is*) sets out from the Snaefellsnes Peninsula.

Hvalstodin (Sea Gannet) (*Reykjavik harbour; tel: 895 2523; www.hafsulan.is*) is one of a number of operators in the capital.

White water or River Rafting

The glaciers that feed Iceland's numerous rivers offer exciting opportunities for white-water rafting whether you can tackle high-category rapids or are just a beginner dipping your toes into the sport for the first time. Boat guides are highly experienced, and companies can cater from easy through moderate to difficult, with the lower age limit ranging from 12 to 18 years.

Arctic Rafting (*Suðerbraut 2, Árnesi, 801 Selfoss; tel: 898 0410; www.arcticrafting.is*) offers trips of varying levels of difficulty.

A whale-watching boat

The Icelandic Horse

The Icelandic horse is classed as a separate breed (*Equus scandinavicus*). Once found all across Scandinavia, as the Latin name suggests, only the Icelandic stock remains pure because it has never been cross-bred like its Norwegian, Swedish and Danish cousins. When the settlers arrived on the island they chose the most hardy horses to make the difficult sea-crossing, keeping the quality of the base population high. Further to this, in 1200 the Alþing passed a law forbidding equine import and export, to protect the bloodline. This makes Icelandic livestock much sought after by today's collectors and prices for fine specimens can run into hundreds of thousands of krona.

One animal that has a place in the hearts of all Icelanders is the horse. Brought by the first Norse settlers they were invaluable for transport and farming, and still serve as a valuable mode of transport for the yearly sheep round-up or réttir.

Despite the farmer's reliance on mechanical machinery and the vast exodus of the population to Reykjavik and its urban surrounds, the horse is thriving and number up to 100,000.

THEY'VE GOT THE MOVES

The Icelandic horse has five gaits, a skill possessed by only one other species – the Mongolian or Prezewalski horse (*Equus prezewalskii*). In addition to the fet (walk), brokk (trot), skeið (canter) and stökk (gallop), the horse also performs a tölt or 'running walk', where the movement is so fluid that the rider doesn't feel any bouncing movement.

Equus scandinavicus is smaller than many breeds, being, in layman's terms, halfway in size between a full-grown horse and a Shetland pony, with an average height of 1.3m at the shoulder. In looks it is gamine of leg and slightly rotund of body, with copious mane and tail to ward off insects and protect it from biting winter winds. Individuals come in a multitude of shades from light champagne beige to jet black.

The breed character is known to be sensible and dependable, so it is perfect for beginners. It is sure-footed, which is ideal for the island's rough terrain.

Many horses are still wild-bred; living out in the hills of the highlands and roaming freely like sheep. They are rounded up each autumn when the year's foals are sold at market.

THE NORSE HORSE

During the Viking era the horse was at once revered yet treated as chattel; and, at times, as a source of food. During the pagan period a prized horse could be buried with his owner or have an epic tale recited in its honour. Conversely, roasted horsemeat was consumed regularly at pagan festivals – when stallions were also pitted against each other for entertainment.

WEATHER VANES

As you travel around the island, watching horses in the field is a good indication of where the prevailing winds are coming from. They have developed a habit of standing rear into the wind with their tails resolutely between their legs to keep delicate parts warm!

Facing page: wild horses grazing in the highlands
Right: the Icelandic horse

Iceland is one of the world's richest birdwatching environments. Although only 70 species breed regularly here, over 300 have been spotted in total. However it is not the number of species but the sheer numbers of individuals that are the draw. The island has an invaluable ecosystem for native, breeding and migratory birds.

WHERE

All the locations mentioned here are easily accessible by road or easy walk, so they are perfect for the fledgling ornithologist or one who doesn't want to have to trek too far and off the beaten path.

Snæfellsnes Peninsula: The southern coast around Arnarstapi is replete with kittiwakes and arctic terns. Guillemots and fulmars breed close by at Þúfubjarg. On the north coast the glaucous gull is more prevalent. At Álftafjörður (Swan Fjord), east of Stykkishólmur, around 500 breeding pairs can be enjoyed.

Reykjanes Peninsula: Just offshore from Reykjanes lighthouse at Elday Island is Iceland's largest gannet colony. Further north at the Hafnaberg cliffs are various species of auk. The northern tip of the peninsula at Garðskagi sees many migratory species in the spring and autumn.

The Westfjords: The Látrabjarg cliffs in the southwest corner are the largest bird-nesting cliffs in Iceland with huge populations of puffins on the flatlands and a razorbill colony at the base.

The north: Lake Mývatn supports vast populations of ducks including Barrow's goldeneye and harlequin, plus grebes, waders and divers.

The East: The marshy delta of the Jökulsá á Dal River offers the largest whimbrel population in Iceland, plus vast flocks of greylag and pink footed geese. Just north of Höfn there is another breeding ground for the whooper swan.

The South: Head to Breiðhamerkursandur to watch the largest great skua colony

on the island, while Dyrhólaey offers puffins, terns and guillemots.

The Westman Islands: The world's largest puffin breeding colony, plus the northernmost breeding ground of Manx shearwater and storm and Leach's petrel.

BIRDWATCHING BY SEASON

Spring: Birds start to stake their claim as early as February but continue to arrive through to the end of May. Cliffs and shorelines are awash with courting pairs while the skies provide an arena for ritual displays. Several species use Iceland as a stopover as they continue north into the Arctic Circle. This is one of the best times to come birdspotting.

Summer: Once breeding is over, many species return to sea and by mid-August the numbers of sea bird drop dramatically. Some species need to spruce up their plumage before winter arrives, so often lie low and are difficult to spot.

Autumn: As the days get shorter, migratory birds tend to gather together in preparation for the flight. Thus geese can be seen roosting in vast numbers inland, while species such as dunlins or sandpipers crowd the coastal shallows. Arctic species also return south for a short pit stop.

Winter: In winter birds move to the coastal fringes to escape the harsh interior. Eiders and gulls are the most common species, but cormorants, skuas and auks can also be seen. The occasional ptarmigan might be viewed inland but snow buntings are more common.

Tip: A pair of binoculars will add immensely to your experience.

Note: Environmental Protection

Iceland has many ground breeding species. Take care to stay on the footpaths when out walking. Some areas are closed during the breeding season. Please abide by local bylaws as these protect delicate breeding grounds.

Facing page above and below:
Birdwatching signs
This page: Watching sea birds

Food and Drink

Iceland has gained a reputation in recent years for fine dining. A generation of young chefs and restaurateurs have taken the modern fusion cuisine that is fashionable at the moment and made it their own. You will certainly be spoilt for choice at the upper end of the quality scale.

A delicious salmon meal

Iceland's natural bounty can be distilled down to three foodstuffs – seafood, lamb and game. This triumvirate forms the basis of almost all the dishes on both traditional and modern menus.

Delicious smoked trout, pan-fried salmon, grilled lobster and fresh sushi make the most of the bounty of the sea. Whale meat can be found on some menus, or you can try *hákarl* (putrified shark) – now considered a delicacy.

You cannot travel anywhere in Iceland without spotting hundreds of sheep. These graze freely on the wild grasses and herbs of the hills and mountains and this imparts a wonderful aromatic flavour to the meat – acting like a natural marinade. Simple grilled lamb is a standard on Icelandic menus but for specialist treats, try *svið* (blackened sheep's head) or *slátur* (parts of sheep minced and stuffed in a sheep's stomach).

Game comes in many forms, some of which may not suit bird lovers. Reindeer is the strong four-legged meat, while sea birds comprise the winged variety with guillemot and puffin being served in a variety of guises – don't forget that Iceland sees millions of these birds throughout the summer, so it is not surprising that they have become an important source of food.

Prices are high by European standards. This is partly explained by the need to import the majority of foodstuffs. Fuel stations around the island offer a good budget eating option. There is always a café on site serving snacks and grill-type meals – they offer good value even if the menu is a little repetitive.

The king of fast food in Iceland is the *pýlsur* – a sausage and bread ensemble much like a hot-dog, with a range of accompaniments from relish to cold, crunchy raw or fried onions. These offer much the best value for a quick lunch or afternoon snack, and you can buy them at kiosks around Reykjavik or at fuel stations.

Drinks

Coffee is king in Iceland and good coffee houses perform the same role as bars or pubs in other countries (*see p152*). *Skyr*, a drink made from skimmed milk flavoured with berries, is very refreshing in summer. Alcohol is very expensive, but not local beers like Gul and Viking or the distilled vodka-like Brennivín that is made from potatoes.

Vegetarians

Reykjavik has a small selection of vegetarian restaurants (*see next page*) which should keep those on a short visit happy, but if you are travelling around the island choice is generally non-existent.

An abundance of fresh vegetables has only arrived in recent years so the Icelandic diet has always focused on meat.

The fish eater won't have a problem as there's always a choice of seafood on any menu – including a lot of delicious sushi – but vegans will have to get creative.

MENU DECODER
Hákarl – putrified shark meat
Hanikjöt – smoked lamb
Harðfiskur – dried haddock eaten as a snack, a little like beef jerky
Karfi – perch
Kartöfl – potatoes
Kjötsúpa – lamb stew
Lundi – puffin
Rauðkál – pickled cabbage
Skyr – a thick drink made from milk and yoghurt culture flavoured with berries
Silð – herring
Skarkoli – plaice
Soðning – boiled fish (served with potatoes)
Slátur – sheep's offal cooked in sheep's stomach
Svið – singed sheep's head cooked and served hot or cold

Enjoying a hearty laugh and drink before beginning the fine dining experience

Prices indicate dinner for one without drinks:

★ under ISK2500
★★ ISK2500–3500
★★★ ISK3500–4500
★★★★ ISK4500 plus

Vegeterians

Á Næstu Grösum ★★
Considered the best of the bunch with a good value set meal daily.
Laugavegur 20b.
Tel: 552 8410.

Café Garðurinn ★
More of a relaxed coffee shop style atmosphere
Klapparstígur 37.
Tel: 561 2345.

Græn Kostur ★
Another informal café with a range of tasty snacks and meals.
Skólavörðustígur 8.
Tel: 552 2028.

Reykjavik

Apótek Bar and Grill ★★★
This old converted pharmacy is now an ultra-modern grill with an open kitchen and soothing white décor. There is a bar/café with windows out onto the main street where you can have snacks and drinks. The restaurant offers great nouvelle Icelandic and inter-national cuisine.
Austurstræti 16.
Tel: 575 7900.
www.veitinar.is

Bæjarins Betzu Pýlsur ★
City dwellers will tell you that this small unassuming kiosk makes the best *pýlsur* in Reykjavik and has been in business since 1935. You may need to queue up but for the tastiest Icelandic hot-dog it's worth it.
Trggvagötu. Tel: 894 4515.

Kaffi Reykjavik ★★★/★★★★
One of the prettiest historic buildings in the downtown core is now a roomy bar/restaurant with an excellent evening seafood buffet, plus a continental/Icelandic à-la-carte menu. You can also enjoy a drink at the Kaffi Reykjavik ice-bar.
Vesturgata 2.
Tel: 552 3030.
www.kaffireykjavik.is

Krua Thai ★★
This canteen-style (no table services) informal eatery services big portions of authentic Thai cuisine – not hot unless you ask for it. It is an inexpensive option and the relaxed environment means that you don't have to be on your best behaviour.
Tryggvagötu 14. Tel: 561 0039. www.kruathai.is

Lækjarbrekka ★★★★
High-class Icelandic cuisine served in a historic timber-clad cottage c1834. The service is impeccable and the food – game and fish – delicious. However, this is one of the most expensive restaurants on the island.
Bankastræti 2.
Tel. 551 4430.
www.laekjarbrekka.is

Perlan ★/★★
The café in the Perlan building is open throughout the day for a good range of fresh salads, sandwiches and items like Belgian waffles and ice cream, plus delicious soups.
Öskjuhlíý. Tel. 562 0200.
Café open: 10am–9pm.

Sjávarkjallarinn ★★★/★★★★
The 'Seafood Cellar' (that is the translation of the restaurant name) is an award-winning restaurant serving Icelandic/Asian fusion cuisine in a cool neon-lit cellar dining room.

Aðalstræti 2.
Tel: 511 1212.
www.sjávarkjallarinn.is

Tapas ★/★★

It may be a surprise to find authentic tapas here but the range is good and you can accompany your meal with a dry sherry or Rioja for the true experience. The basement dining room is wood-panelled with booth seating. Good atmosphere and friendly service.
Vesturgata 3b.
Tel: 551 2344.

Rest of the Island

Bautinn ★/★★★

A good and popular reasonably budget option in the centre of town,

Bautinn offers snacks and fast food (burgers etc), a salad buffet and a range of full meals. A good family option.
Hafnastræti 92, Akureyri.
Tel: 462 1818.
www.bautinn.is

Cowshed Café ★

This small café has been built in a section of a farm's cowshed and you can watch the milking through large picture windows. It serves a range of sandwiches and snacks including huge portions of cheesecake and bread cooked in geothermic heat. There is a terrace to enjoy the weather in summer.
Vogafjos. Tel: 464 4303.

A fish buffet at Kaffi Reykjavik

Gamli Baukur ★★/★★★

This timber chalet down on the harbour is always busy around lunch time with people embarking and disembarking from whale-watching trips – the terrace is a great place to watch the harbour sea-traffic come and go. The menu has soups, salads and main courses, concentrating on seafood.
Hafn, Húsavík.
Tel: 464 2442.
www.gamlibaukur.is

Sjávarloftið ★★★

The restaurant's name means ocean floor and the menu concentrates on fruits of the sea. The dining room is a warm but modern wooden-clad loft area, while the ground floor is a popular and informal café.
Aðalgötu 3, Stykkishólmur.
Tel: 438 1119.

Systra Kaffi ★★/★★★

Excellent but very busy café/restaurant serving a range of snacks and main meals plus very generous pizzas (large and small). A good choice for breakfast, lunch or dinner.
Klausturvegur,
Kirkjubæjarklauster.
Tel: 487 4848.

Hotels and Accommodation

Accommodation in Iceland is expensive by European standards and the hotel industry is still developing. Most of the upmarket hotels are to be found in the capital. There are a small number of comfortable properties scattered around the island, backed up by seasonal B&Bs and guesthouses.

Hotel Edda Hellissandur

Edda Hotels

These hotels (*www.hoteledda.is*) started out using the rooms of students in boarding schools for visitor accommodation in summer. Many also have 'sleeping bag space,' for those who carry their own bedding. Recently the group has branched out into custom-built hotel properties, often in more remote parts of the island.

For hotel accommodation it is important to make a booking during July and August, as space is limited. B&B accommodation is plentiful in Reykjavik but the standards vary. Prices are highest in summer and can drop by 40 per cent in winter.

Prices

Peak season prices per room:

★	Under ISK9000
★★	ISK9000–13000
★★★	Over 13000

Reykjavik

Domus Guesthouse ★
The former Norwegian Embassy has been turned into a stylish B&B with nice furniture and an upmarket ambience.
Hvertisgata 45.
Tel: 561 1200.

Gistiheimilið Sunna ★
A very central guesthouse in the shadow of the cathedral and within walking distance of all that the city has to offer.
Þórsgata 26. Tel: 551 5570.
www.sunna.is

Hotel Loftleiðir ★★★
The refurbished Loftleiður sits close to Perlan and was once the hotel attached to the international airport – now the domestic airport. The 220 rooms are divided into four standards including a number dedicated to Icelandic poets.

There is a swimming pool, sauna and gym, and a shuttle bus to the city centre.
v/Hlíðarflót, 101 Reykjavik. Tel: 444 4500.
www.icehotels.is

Nordica Hotel ★★★
The flagship of the Icehotel chain, the Nordica is one of the most stylish hotels on the island. The rooms have a cool Scandinavian feel and there is a top-class spa and the gourmet VOX restaurant on site. The hotel lies a five-minute car journey from the city

centre but there is a shuttle bus.
Suðurlandsbraut 2, 108 Reykjavik. Tel: 444 5000.
www.icehotels.is

Around Reykjavik
Hotel Flúðir ★★/★★★
Set in Icelands 'golden circle', the Flúðir is a single-storey, chalet-style hotel with small but well furnished rooms each leading out onto a small terrace. The relaxing restaurant offers Icelandic specialities, and vegetables grown in the surrounding countryside.

Vesterbrún 1, 845 Fluðir. Tel: 486 6630.
www.icehotels.is

Flughótel ★★★
This 42-room modern hotel in the heart of Keflavik is close to the Blue Lagoon and perfect for stay while touring the Reykjanes Peninsula, or as a last-night stay as it is a short drive away from the international airport.
There is a hotpot, sauna, massage and fitness room on site, plus an informal eatery serving meals and snacks throughout the day.

Hafnargata 57, 230 Keflavik. Tel: 421 5222.
www.icehotels.is

Fire and Ice Guesthouse ★
Frost og Funi, or Fire and Ice, owns three different properties. Each is a guesthouse with various levels of facilities. The Hveragerdi property sits on the banks of a river and has bright modern rooms, pool and hotpot, and serves organic breakfasts.
Hverlamar, Hveragerdi. Tel: 483 4959.
www.frostogfuni.is

Entrance of the Nordica Hotel

Hotel Hérað

Northwest
Hotel Edda
Hellissandur ★★
A modern custom-built hotel that offers the most luxurious option for a stay on the Snæfellsnes Peninsula. The rooms are light and airy with 'Scandinavian' styling, and there is a decent restaurant and small bar on site. Good views of Snæfellsjökull in good weather *(open: all year) Klettsbúð 9.*
Tel: 444 4940.

Hotel Edda Ísafjörður ★★
A range of accommodation: 10 suites, 30 rooms with basin, sleeping bag space and an area allotted for tents. The price range is for rooms with private facilities (*Open: Jun–late Aug) Menntaskólinn.*
Tel: 444 4960.

North
Edda Hotel Akureyri ★★
This ultramodern hotel offers 118 three-star rooms all the year round; in summer there are non-en-suite rooms and sleeping bag space in the dorm section of the school that occupies the same site. There is a restaurant on site.
(*Price range for rooms with private facilities. Open: mid Jun–end Aug.) Eyarlandsvegur 28.*
Tel: 444 4900.

Gistiheimilið Árból ★
The lovely 100-year-old timber mansion which is now a guesthouse has great character with pretty rooms and a garden with a river at the end.
Ásgarðsvegur 2, Húsavík. Tel: 464 2220.

Eldá ★
This company runs several B&Bs and self-catering cottages around Lake Mývatn. They are good for birdwatching or fishing trips or when simply passing through on an around-the-island tour. It also operates tours and excursions in the region.
Helluhraun 15, Mývatn. Tel: 464 2220.
www.elda.is

East
Hotel Hérað ★★★
The modern Hérað has comfortable modern rooms, and there is a good bar with a small terrace outside and a excellent restaurant on site. Ideally situated for touring the Eastfjords, it is a pleasant retreat after a day's exploration.
Miðvanger 5–7, 770 Edgilsstaðir. Tel: 471 1500.
www.icelhotels.is

Hotel Tangi ★★
A surprising find in a tiny Eastfjords town, the 14 rooms have clean modern

lines and there is a good restaurant/bar on site. From here you can set out to explore some of the least visited regions of the island.
Hafnarbyggð 17, Vopnaðfjörður. Tel: 473 1224.

South
Edda Skógar ★
Sitting next door to the Skógar Museum, this summer hotel has 34 rooms but with non-en-suite bathrooms. The hotel offers a dinner buffet and has an indoor pool and outdoor hotpot (*open: Jun-end Aug*).
861 Hvolsvöllur. Tel: 444 4830.

Hotel Edda Vik I Mýrdal ★/★★
This modern, single-storey hotel is only minutes from the black beach and volcanic cliffs of Vik. There is a restaurant on site. It has 21 rooms (*open: May–end-Aug*).
v/Klettsveg, Vik. Tel: 444 4840.

Hotel Klauster ★★/★★★
Suitably situated on the route between Reykjavik and the Skaftafell National Park and a perfect stop on the round-Iceland circuit, the Klauster has 57 nicely furnished rooms.
Klaustervegur 6,
Kirkjubæjarklauster. Tel: 487 4900. www.icehotels.is

Hotel Rangá ★★★
Iceland's second four-star property offers a total contrast to the Nordica in Reykjavik, being in the heart of the countryside surrounded by good fishing and several golf courses.

The wooden chalet-style property is almost Alpine in character; the restaurant has an excellent wine list and there is a cigar bar on site.
Suðurlandsvegur, 851 Hella. Tel: 487 5700. www.icehotels.isa

Camping at Flúðir

Practical Guide

Arriving
Entry Formalities
Citizens of the following countries can enter Iceland without a visa provided their passport is valid for three months after the end of their stay – EU countries, Australia, Canada, New Zealand, Switzerland, Great Britain (including Bermuda, Turks and Caicos Islands, Cayman Islands, Anguilla, Montserrat, British Virgin Islands, St. Helena, Falkland Islands and Gibraltar), United States of America.

Visas
Foreign citizens who must produce a visa upon arrival in Iceland, now also gain entry to the other Schengen countries. All countries who have signed up to the Shengen Agreement allow free movement of their peoples between each country without having to show passports at the borders of frontiers.

Schengen visas should be obtained prior to arrival in the Schengen territory. In most instances, Danish embassies will handle visa applications on behalf of Iceland. A list of these embassies and further information is available on the Directorate of Immigration home page, *www.utl.is*

Arriving by Air
The main airport of entry is Keflavik (*tel: 425 0777; www.keflavikairport.com*), 40km southwest of Reykjavik.

Scheduled flights: Icelandair (*www.icelandair.com*) is the national carrier offering a network of services to major cities throughout western Europe and northern USA. There are no direct flights from Australia or New Zealand to Iceland. Multiple ticket combinations for flights into Europe and onward to Reykjavik are possible.

Flybus links the international airport

Icelandic aircraft

at Keflavik with Reykjavik. They are timed to meet all incoming flights.

Arriving by Sea

Smyril Line runs a weekly 1500-vehicle ferry all the year round linking Seyðisfjörður on the east coast of Iceland, the Faroe Islands, the Shetland Islands, Sweden and Denmark. From mainland Britain there are ferry connections via Smyril Lines ferries from Aberdeen to the Faroe Islands. Contact Smyril Line Faroe Islands (*PO Box 370, FR 110 Tórshavn; tel: 298 315 900 www.smyril-line.fo*) for details. *See also Public transport, bus and ferry timetables p188.*

Camping

Camping is popular, and there are sites in most towns and in national parks and areas of natural beauty. Some farms also offer camping space. Facilities at most sites are basic with a small toilet/shower block and a couple of sinks. Power is not normally provided. Sites may become overcrowded in high season (June–August). Most sites are close to small supermarkets where you can buy provisions. Most camp sites close mid-September to the end of May. There are 29 motorhome waste dump sites around the island, situated at camp sites and some fuel stations.

For more details, contact the Iceland Environment and Food Agency (*Suðurlandsbraut 24, 108 Reykjavik; tel: 591 2000; www.ust.is*).

Children

Make sure that children are adequately protected against the weather. In cold weather have hat and gloves ready, plus a waterproof and warm outer layer. In sunny weather, protect their skin with high-factor cream even if the temperature doesn't seem warm.

Climate

Despite its northerly position, the coastline of Iceland has a remarkably mild climate. It benefits from the Gulf Stream that keeps the air relatively benign – cool in summer and mild in winter.

In summer the average temperature is 51°F with warmer spells sometimes. In winter temperatures average at around freezing point (comparable to New York). At all times of the year the weather can change frequently. (*Weather information in English: tel: 902 0600 ext 44; www.vedur.is*)

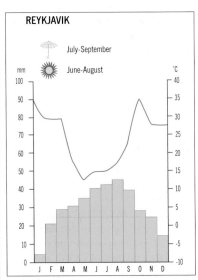

REYKJAVIK

July-September

June-August

Weather Conversion Chart
25.4mm = 1 inch
°F = 1.8 x °C + 32

Crime

When you visit Iceland you are at relatively low risk of being a victim of serious crime. However, so-called petty crime such as theft can be a problem in Reykjavik, especially from vehicles. Crime is almost non-existent in the small towns in the rest of the island. Precautions to minimise your chances of a loss include:

Do not leave valuables in a car and leave nothing on display.

Don't carry large amounts of cash or valuables with you.

Deposit valuables in the hotel safe. Take extra care at cash point machines – don't allow bystanders to see your PIN.

Don't leave valuables unattended in cafés and restaurants.

Customs regulations

The following duty-free rules apply:
Over-20s are allowed to take in the following items duty free:
1 litre of wine or 6 litres of beer
1 litre of stronger alcohol
If no spirits and beer, then 2.5 litres of wine can be imported.
Over-18s can also take 200 cigarettes or 250g of tobacco
There are no currency restrictions.

Driving

Driving around in Iceland can be a challenge but is generally not difficult provided you exercise care and caution. Roads are a mixture of asphalt and compacted dirt surfaces and you may pass from one to the other regularly – the transition area between the two (signposted *Malbik endar*) requires extra care.

Iceland drives on the right, overtaking on the left. Speed limits are 50kph in urban areas, 80kph on gravel roads and 90kph on asphalt surfaces, but in some local streets speeds may drop to 30kph. Speed bumps are common at town limits. It is forbidden to drive off prescribed roads and lanes.

Seat belts are compulsory for all passengers including passengers on tour buses. Headlights must be on at all times when the vehicle is in motion (day or night). Motorists are not allowed to drive after drinking alcohol and the law is strictly enforced.

Most bridges on the island are single-lane (signposted *Einbreið brú*) and when oncoming traffic approaches it is the first car there that has priority. If in any doubt, let oncoming traffic have priority.

On dirt roads, traffic normally rides in the middle of the road until other traffic approaches, so flying stones can be a problem when overtaking or passing oncoming traffic.

Welcome sign at the Port of Reykjavik

There are many blind rises on roads (signposted *Blindhæd*). Make sure you keep to the right when approaching these crests.

Look out for fast-moving four-wheel-drive trucks or slow-moving farm vehicles. Sheep wander freely, so slow down as you approach them. Also, slow down for people on horseback.

A special mention must be made about the highland roads of the interior. These must not be attempted in a two-wheel-drive vehicle as the surfaces and ground clearances are not suitable.

Weather is a major factor when driving in Iceland. Rain and ice can make road surfaces slippery and low cloud can shorten visibility, especially on mountain passes. Roads can be closed because of weather conditions at all times of year and closed throughout the winter (October-May), so ask about the conditions before travelling.

For information on current conditions of all Iceland's roads (*tel: 354 1777; www.vegagerdin.is*). For weather information in English (*tel: 902 0600*).

Fuel

Most major towns have a choice of fuel stations while smaller settlements have one source – this usually comes with a general store and café. Note that a small number of fuel stations do not have a store/café. You will only be able to pay for fuel by credit card or fuel card (ISK 3000 or ISK 5000) at the pump – the fuel cards are for sale in the store. Fuel can be purchased after hours via the credit card machine at the pump. Keep your vehicle well fuelled as distances between pumps can be long.

Conversion Table

FROM	TO	MULTIPLY BY
Inches	Centimetres	2.54
Feet	Metres	0.3048
Yards	Metres	0.9144
Miles	Kilometres	1.6090
Acres	Hectares	0.4047
Gallons	Litres	4.5460
Ounces	Grams	28.35
Pounds	Grams	453.6
Pounds	Kilograms	0.4536
Tons	Tonnes	1.0160

To convert back, for example from centimetres to inches, divide by the number in the third column.

Men's Suits

UK	36	38	40	42	44	46	48
Iceland & Rest of Europe	46	48	50	52	54	56	58
USA	36	38	40	42	44	46	48

Dress Sizes

UK	8	10	12	14	16	18
France	36	38	40	42	44	46
Italy	38	40	42	44	46	48
Iceland & Rest of Europe	34	36	38	40	42	44
USA	6	8	10	12	14	16

Men's Shirts

UK	14	14.5	15	15.5	16	16.5	17
Iceland & Rest of Europe	36	37	38	39/40	41	42	43
USA	14	14.5	15	15.5	16	16.5	17

Men's Shoes

UK	7	7.5	8.5	9.5	10.5	11
Iceland & Rest of Europe	41	42	43	44	45	46
USA	8	8.5	9.5	10.5	11.5	12

Women's Shoes

UK	4.5	5	5.5	6	6.5	7
Iceland & Rest of Europe	38	38	39	39	40	41
USA	6	6.5	7	7.5	8	8.5

Tourist Office in Reykjavik

Car Rental

Cars can be rented at Keflavik airport, in Reykjavik or at domestic airports. A four-wheel-drive vehicle is advised because it gives you extra grip on the gravel roads but if you intend to travel into the highlands, four-wheel-drive is compulsory to cope with the rough conditions. Note that if you rent a two-wheel-drive vehicle and attempt routes only suitable for four-wheel-drive vehicles, your car insurance will become void. If you rent a four-wheel-drive vehicle your insurance is not valid for fording water.

There are local and international agencies but the company with the largest network is Hertz. They have offices at most major centres and offer the best back-up if you have a problem.

Your domestic driving licence is recognised in Iceland. You will need to have had a full license for at least one year and be over 21 to rent a vehicle; most rental companies require you to be 23 to rent a four-wheel-drive vehicle.

You will need a credit card to stand for a deposit.

Bringing your own vehicle into Iceland
Carry the registration document, valid insurance and valid licence. A temporary import permit valid for one month will be issued at your port of entry. This can be extended.

Electricity

Iceland uses 240v 50hz for its supply. Plugs are the two-pinned variety, so travellers from the UK will need an adaptor.

Embassies

Embassies located in Reykjavik:
UK *Laufásvegur 31, 101 Reykjavik. Postal address – PO Box 460, 121 Reykjavik. Tel: 550 5100; fax: 550 5105. www.britishembassy.is*
Vice Consul – Akureyri *Central Hospital (Fjordungssjukrahusid a Akureyri), v/Eyrarlandsveg. Postal address – PO Box 380, I S 602 Akureyri. Tel: 463 0102; fax: 462 4621.*
US Embassy *Laufásvegur 21, 101 Reykjavik. Tel: 562 9100; fax: 562 1020. www.usa.is*
Australian Embassy
No Australian Embassy or Consul
Canadian Embassy *Túngata 14. Postal address – PO Box 1510, 101 Reykjavik.*

Tel: 575 6500; fax: 575 6501.
www.canada.is

Republic of Ireland Honorary Consulate
Mr David Thorsteinsson, Ásbuð 106,
Gardabaer. Tel: 554 2355; fax: 568 6564.

New Zealand
No embassy or consular representation

South Africa Honorary Consul
Borgatún 35. Postal address: PO Box 462,
105 Reykjavik. Tel: 591 0355;
fax: 354 591 0358.

Emergency telephone numbers
For Ambulance, Fire and Police,
available 24 hours a day, telephone 112.

Health
There are no compulsory inoculations
for travel to Iceland. Medical provision
is of a high standard with all staff
speaking some English if not good
English, but charges are expensive. Small
settlements will have a local clinic and
large towns a hospital.

UK and EU citizens must produce
an European Health Insurance Card,
available online at www.ehic.org.uk,
by phoning 0845 6062030 or from
post offices, in order to obtain
free treatment; otherwise they
will be charged and will need
to reclaim the money on
their return.

Citizens of other
countries must pay at the
time of treatment in local
currency (take receipts to
claim money back from
your insurance company)
unless they have insurance
with a company that pays
direct.

Pharmacies (*apótek*) sell many drugs
over the counter; however, brand names
vary, so if you need a specific
medication/drug take an empty packet
with you to aid the pharmacist or carry
a prescription from your doctor.

Insurance
Having adequate insurance cover is vital
– see Health above. UK citizens with a
European Health Insurance Card will be
treated without charge but a travel
insurance policy will allow repatriation
if the injuries/illness warrants it. All
other nationalities should ensure
adequate cover for illness, as they will be
charged at the point of treatment.

Travellers should always have cover
for everything they carry with them in
case of loss or theft.

Insurance companies also usually
provide cover for cancellation or travel
delay. Though not essential, this cover
offers some compensation if travel
plans go awry.

Lost property
Icelanders are by nature very
honest people and will hand
lost items in at cafes etc., so
retrace your steps if you can,
to see if your item can be
found. If not, try the local
police station. You will need
an official police report to
make an insurance claim for
any lost property. If you
lose your passport, contact
your Embassy or Consulate
immediately.

Narrow bridge road sign

Icelandic newspaper

Language

The national language of Iceland is Icelandic, a Scandinavian language with Germanic roots. But don't worry – almost all Icelanders speak good English.

Maps

Most tourist offices produce good maps of their towns and regions for car tours. If you intend to do any hiking, a specialist map is advised. Landmælinger Íslands produce accurate ones for the whole of the island.

Media

Iceland has three TV channels. Many programmes are broadcast in their native language with Icelandic subtitles, so there are lots of UK and American favourites. Large hotels have satellite TV, usually with CNN, BBC News 24 or Sky News channels.

There are no English-language mainstream newspapers printed in Iceland. International papers are available in newsagents/bookstores at Reykjavik and Akureryri.

Internet cafés and WiFi hotspots are common.

Money Matters
Money

The Icelandic currency is the Icelandic Króna, usually indicated by the initials ISK. Coins come in denominations of 100 kr., 50 kr., 10kr., 5 kr. and 1 kr., and bank notes in denominations of 5000 kr., 2000 kr.,1000 kr., and 500 kr.

All Icelandic banks provide foreign exchange. They are found in all major

PRONUNCIATION

All letters are pronounced as in English unless indicated below.

Capital	small case	Pronunciation
Ð	ð	'th' as in feather
Þ	þ	'th' as in thing
Ý or Í	ý or í	'ee'
Á	á	'ow'
É	é	'ye' as in yes
Ó	ó	'o' as in wrote
Ö	ö	'e' as in stern
Æ	æ	'eye'
AU	au	'ur' of furry without the r
Ú	ú	The 'oo' of true
J	j	As 'y' in yes
DJ	dj	Hard j sound
F	f	As in English, but also 'v' in vain. Pronounced as an abrupt 'b' before an l or an n
HV	hv	kv
LL	ll	As in the 'ddl' in riddle
P	p	As in English but pronounced 'f' if before an s or a t
R	r	Always rolled on the tongue

HELPFUL PHRASES

English	Icelandic
Hello	Hállo
Goodbye	Bless
Yes	Jái
No	Nei
Do you speak English?	Talar þu ensku?
I don't understand	Ég skil ekki
Where is the?	Hvar er?
How much is it?	Hvar koster petta?
Thank you	Takk fyrir
Do you have any vacancies?	Eru herbergi laus?
My name is	Ég heiti
Doctor	lækni
Dentist	tannlæknir
Tourist office	Upplýsingaþjónustu fyrir ferðafólk
Help!	Hjálp!

One	einn
Two	tveir
Three	þrír
Four	fjórir
Five	fimm
Six	sex
Seven	sjö
Eight	átta
Nine	níu
Ten	tíu
One hundred	Eitt hundrað

Information

Austurvöllur

Ráðhús

Tjörnin

towns and are generally open on weekdays from 9.15am to 4pm. Travellers will find it easier if they carry US Dollars, Euros or Pounds Sterling, which are easier to change than other currencies.

Hotels may provide an exchange service but their commission rates are expensive.

Traveller's cheques: Not as easy to cash as foreign currency, they can only be changed at banks (though they are more secure than cash as you can get them replaced if they get lost or stolen)

ATM: ATMs are becoming more numerous and you will certainly be able to get cash in all the major Icelandic towns.

Credit cards

Credit cards are widely accepted across Iceland, and locals use plastic for even the smallest purchases. The most popular ones are MasterCard and Visa. You can use your credit card to get cash advances over the counter in banks.

Opening hours

Shops are open Monday–Friday 9am–6pm, Saturday 10am–4pm with extended hours in summer and in shopping malls in Reykjavik. Some souvenir shops in Reykjavik and the shopping malls are open on Sundays 10am–6pm. Supermarkets are open 9am–9pm and some until 11pm. Banks remain open Monday–Friday 9.15am–4pm.

Icelandic Police Officer

Museums have varying opening hours because many are private. Museums in the capital are generally open Monday–Friday 9am–5pm, Saturday–Sunday noon–5pm. Other museums are open June–September but, check hours within this guide.

Pharmacies, as for shops. There are duty pharmacies in the major towns.

Mail Box

Police

Police wear navy-blue uniforms and routinely carry guns. They are generally approachable for queries such as asking directions and most speak good English. The emergency telephone number is 112.

Post Offices

Postal services are operated by the state-run HP recognised by their red signs and post boxes. Main post offices are open Monday–Friday 9am–4.30pm. Smaller offices around the island may open slightly longer or shorter hours. In addition to this, in Reykjavik the post office at Grensásvegur 9 is open on Saturday 10am–2pm, and the post office at Þönglabakki 4 is open Monday–Friday 10am–6pm.

Public Holidays

The following dates are official holidays in Iceland – most dates are moveable, so check with the tourist office before you travel. All government buildings and banks and most commercial businesses will be closed on these days.

1 January
New Year's Day
March/April
Maundy Thursday
March/April
Good Friday
March/April
Easter Sunday
March/April
Easter Monday
April/early-May
First Day of summer
1 May Labour Day
Mid–late-May Ascension Day
Mid-May–early-June Whit Sunday
Mid-May–early-June Whit Monday
17th June National Day
Early-August Bank Holiday Monday
24th December Christmas Eve
(from midday)
25th December Christmas Day
26th December Boxing Day
31st December New Year's Eve
(from midday)

Public transport
Air

Local air services run by Air Iceland operate from Reykjavik to nine settlements around the island with airfields at Akureyri, Egilsstaðir, Grímsey, Hornafjörður, Ísafjörður, Vopnafjörður and Þóshöfn. There are also combination air and bus vouchers with one way by air and return by bus. Routes are from the hub at Reykjavik.

Bus

In Reykjavik buses run Monday–Saturday from 7am–midnight and Sunday from 10am–midnight.

Bus services offer an efficient method of touring around and even run trips into the Highlands during the summer, though distances and times can be long. Destination Iceland (*Lágmúli 4, Reykjavik; tel: 354 585 4270; www.dice.is*) offers several types of passes or vouchers for touring the whole island or separate regions.

Ferry

A well-managed fleet of ferries link the mainland outlying islands the year round. Details can be got from the harbour offices.

Bus and Ferry Timetables

The Thomas Cook European Rail Timetable is published monthly and gives the times of buses and ferries in Iceland. It is available to buy online at *www.thomascookpublishing.com*, from branches of Thomas Cook in the UK or by phoning *01733 416477*.

Sustainable Tourism

Thomas Cook is a strong advocate of ethical and fairly traded tourism and believes that the travel experience should be as good for the places visited as it is for the people that visit. That's why we're a firm supporter of The Travel Foundation: a charity that develops solutions to help improve and protect holiday destinations, their environment, traditions and culture. To find out what you can do to make a positive difference to the places you travel to and the people who live there, please visit *www.thetravelfoundation.org.uk*

Telephones

Modern hotels usually have a direct dial phone system, but beware as they often charge huge surcharges to make calls. Ask about charges before you decide to ring home.

The country code for Iceland is 354, all numbers have seven digits and there is no need to dial the country code once you are on the island.

Here are the main country codes, should you want to make an international call from Iceland.

USA and Canada 00 1
UK 00 44
Ireland 00 353
Australia 00 61
New Zealand 00 64

Siminn is the main service provider, though the opening of

Road Rule sign

Take a ferry ride to the islands

the market in 2005 means more competition for the future.

Time

Iceland operates Greenwich Mean Time throughout the year, so in winter, if it is midday in Reykjavik it is the same time in London, 5am in New York and Toronto. In summer it is 1pm in London, 6am in New York or Toronto.

Tipping

Tipping is not expected in Iceland.

Toilets

Toilets are generally clean and of a good standard. There are public facilities at all fuel stations and information centres. National parks and rural car parks also have toilets. In urban areas, visit a café/bar.

Tourist information

Every town has a well-equipped and helpful Tourist Information office that will help with information about excursions and accommodation. The Reykjavik offices also give a lot of information about other parts of the island.

The website *www.visiticeland.com* is an excellent source of information.

Travellers with disabilities

Provision for travellers with mobility problems is variable. New buildings have to meet a code of standard for wheelchair access. Always make specific enquiries at hotels if you require specially equipped rooms. Because of the very nature of its natural attractions, some areas of beauty with be difficult to access.

For more holiday and travel information for people with disabilities, contact Holiday Care Services (*tel: 0845 124 9971 (UK); www.holidaycare. org.uk*).

ACKNOWLEDGEMENTS
The writer and photographer would like to send thanks to Hjörvar S. Högnason of Icelandair UK and Dóra Magnúsdóttir at Visit Reykjavik for their invaluable help and enthusiasm during the research for this book.

Thomas Cook Publishing wishes to thank Pete Bennett, Big World Productions for the photographs in this book, to whom the copyright in the photographs belongs.

Send your thoughts to
books@thomascook.com

We're committed to providing the very best up-to-date information in our travel guides and constantly strive to make them as useful as they can be. You can help us to improve future editions by letting us have your feedback. If you've made a wonderful discovery on your travels that we don't already feature, if you'd like to inform us about recent changes to anything that we do include, or if you simply want to let us know your thoughts about this guidebook and how we can make it even better – we'd love to hear from you.

Send us ideas, discoveries and recommendations today and then look out for your valuable input in the next edition of this title. And, as an extra 'thank you' from Thomas Cook Publishing, you'll be automatically entered into our exciting monthly prize draw.

Emails to the above address, or letters to Travellers Project Editor, Thomas Cook Publishing, PO Box 227, Unit 18, Coningsby Road, Peterborough PE3 8SB, UK.

Please don't forget to let us know which title your feedback refers to!

FOR LABURNUM TECHNOLOGIES

Design Director	Alpana Khare	**Designer**	Neeraj Aggarwal
Series Director	Sunanda Lahiri	**DTP Designer**	Manish Aggarwal
Editor	Indira Chandrashekar	**Photo Editor**	Manju Singhal

Thanks to Bikram Grewal for the index.